THE BORDER TERRIER

THE
BORDER
TERRIER

By

ANNE ROSLIN - WILLIAMS

Illustrated with
16 *Plates of Photographs*

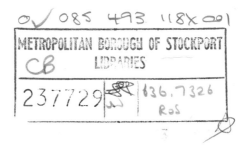
H. F. & G. WITHERBY LTD.

FIRST PUBLISHED IN 1976
BY H. F. & G. WITHERBY LTD
5 PLANTAIN PLACE, CROSBY ROW,
LONDON, SE1 1YN.

ISBN 0 85493 118 X

Printed in Great Britain by
WITHERBY & CO. LTD.
Aylesbury Street, London, EC1

*Dedicated
to all
Border Terrier Fans*

CONTENTS

For map showing Redesdale and Coquetdale see overleaf

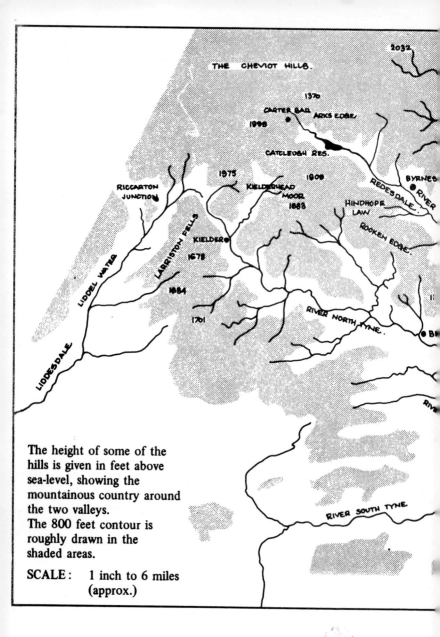

THE CHEVIOT HILLS.

2032

1370

CARTER BAR
ARKS EDGE.
1998

CATCLEUGH RES.

RICCARTON
JUNCTION

1975

KIELDERHEAD
MOOR
1883

1908

BYRNES
RIVER

REDESDALE

HINDHOPE
LAW

ROOKEN EDGE.

LIDDEL WATER

LARRISTON FELLS

KIELDER
1678

1884

1701

RIVER NORTH TYNE.

B

LIDDESDALE

RIV

The height of some of the
hills is given in feet above
sea-level, showing the
mountainous country around
the two valleys.
The 800 feet contour is
roughly drawn in the
shaded areas.

SCALE :   1 inch to 6 miles
           (approx.)

RIVER SOUTH TYNE

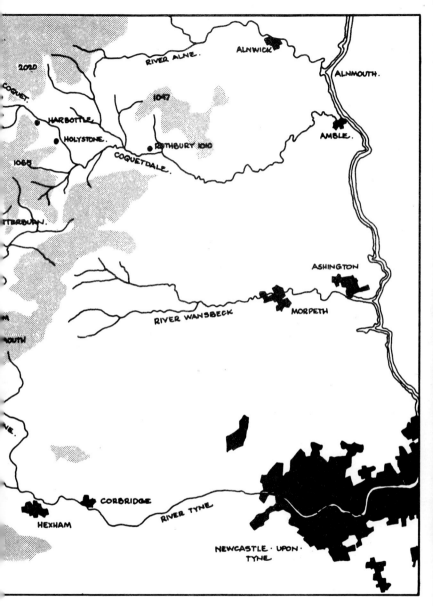

MAP SHOWING REDESDALE AND COQUETDALE

LIST OF PHOTOGRAPHS

Between Pages

ACKNOWLEDGEMENTS

I would like to express my thanks to The Kennel Club for permission to reproduce the Breed Standard, and to Mr. D. P. Todd for his kindness in allowing me to include his poem *The Terrier Song*. My thanks are also due to Frank Jackson for drawing the map of Redesdale and Coquetdale, to Jill Bower for the drawing on the spine of the book jacket and to The Southern Border Terrier Club for granting me access to Miss Garnett-Orme's records.

For the photographs, acknowledgements and thanks are due to the following:

Mrs. Wendy Smith for 4, Frank Meads for 11, Thomas Fall for 17 and 18 and Gordon Melrose for 26. The Cotswold Wildlife Park, Burford, for permission to use 4; Mrs. Marchant for supplying 2, Mrs. Adam Forster 3, Mr. Roy Thompson 13 and 14, Mr. Gardiner 19, Mrs. Mulcaster 21, Mrs. Cuddigan 22 and Mrs. John T. Renton 23. For permission to photograph "Nellie" I am indebted to Mr. and Mrs. Ben Johnson.

With the exception of 16 and 27 all the other photographs, including "Nellie", have been taken by me. My photograph on the book jacket depicts Ch. Dandyhow Shady Knight with one of his famous daughters, Ch. Dandyhow Burnished Silver.

A.R-W.

xi

INTRODUCTION

No excuse should be needed to write about the breed one loves but my excuse, or rather cause, was the visit of my mother to Kenya, during which fortnight I had nothing to do but look after her dogs. The challenge had already been presented to me by a publisher who suggested such a book, and then back-pedalled, saying that there was no interest in the breed. This really annoyed me as I thought of the great number of Border Terrier fans that I had met in this country either working or showing their dogs, or living with them as dearly loved and much respected companions and pals, and also my many friends in the breed overseas. With help and encouragement from the small handful of people who I took into my confidence, I laboured on to produce a book which I hope will be of interest, in some part at least, to all those who admire the breed.

Of necessity, a large part of this book applies chiefly to the show Border, but as there is no separation, and I hope there never will be, of the showdog from the working dog, I hope that the point will be taken that my remarks apply to the Border Terrier as a breed, not just to one side of it.

The past history of the breed was primarily that of a working terrier which then found its way into the show-ring, but still retained all the attributes of the working terrier. At the present time this still applies. The future of the breed could well be affected by anti-hunting laws which may be passed in the not too distant future. If and when that black day should come, those of us

1

who have been fortunate in knowing the breed at work must strive to see that none of the working characteristics are lost. Should they be lost the breed would become just another showdog and smartness and showmanship would be prized more highly than true breed type, character and brains. Let us hope this day never comes, as I, for one, will have no further interest in the Border should the 'essence' of the breed be lost—that the Border Terrier is essentially a working terrier.

I would like to record my personal gratitude, apart from to all those who have encouraged me over this book, to those people who were so helpful to me when I was a raw beginner, and very young, as well as very green. To Mr. and Mrs. Leatt, Mrs. Holmes and Mr. Brown my special thanks.

My start into the breed may interest others who are just beginning. My father always had a large pack of working terriers of varying types and breeds, apart from the gundogs. The day he was given a Border Terrier I decided that these were my breed. That dog later became a famous worker, Smuts, born 1948, who appears often in this book, and later my first show dog. Another Border was added, Red Squill, born 1952, another good worker. She appeared in the show-ring on several occasions with my mother handling her, as I was too shy! Eventually my mother tricked me into appearing in the ring, and away I went—bitten by the bug. As my father hunted the Kendal and District Otterhounds for many seasons and was also a keen follower of the Lunesdale Foxhounds, I was already well into the working side from my earliest memories. Squill died at a relatively early age and I wanted a good show Border. Mr. and Mrs. Leatt offered me the choice of three lovely bitches. I chose Leatty Juliet of Law and made her a Champion very quickly: although technically owned by mother, she was actually mine, as were all the Borders following her. To encourage any younger enthusiasts let me tell them that I handled her to her title when I was eighteen. Mrs. Leatt kept

2

another of the three bitches which became Ch. Leatty Loyallass, and the third one became a Champion overseas—what a wonderful choice they offered me. Mrs. Holmes also offered me the choice of two lovely bitches, both already Champions, as brood bitches: Ch. Wharfholm Winnie and Ch. Warfholm Wink—a terrible decision to choose between two such lovely bitches, but I eventually chose Wink as she was the younger of the two. Sadly, I lost Wink whelping, whereupon Mrs. Holmes let me have the puppy she had kept for herself and was just about to start to show, which later became Ch. Mansergh Wharfholm Wistful. Mr. Brown, who bred Ch. Leatty Juliet of Law, helped me so much by teaching me how to present her properly for show, and by encouraging me all the while.

Borders have given me so much pleasure, firstly by being just Border Terriers in their every day life; secondly as sporting terriers; and lastly as a challenging show dog —not easy to breed, prepare or show—but when a good dog is acknowledged by the magic word 'Champion', or by topping an Any Variety Class, it is all worth while.

In the following chapters I have tried to present the Border Terrier as I know it, presenting the disadvantages of the breed as well as the special attributes which it undoubtedly has retained through the years. Over the years I have been asked many questions about the breed by people interested in purchasing a Border Terrier. These questions I answer truthfully and to the best of my ability, so that a prospective owner of a Border will know what to expect. The answers given appear in this book and I sincerely hope that I have not been misleading about the breed in any way.

Whatever their interest in the breed may be, Border Terrier people the world over are one vast clan, and all devoted to these interesting and game little terriers. It is my hope that every Border fan who reads this book will find something to interest them therein. It has certainly fascinated me to write it.

CHAPTER 1

The Breed Character

The rather special character of the Border must fill those who understand these little dogs with respect and admiration. To those who have never been lucky enough to own one the Border may seem to be a rather nondescript little dog, something between a mongrel and a Griffon. However, those who have once owned the breed usually continue to own them for ever, such is the charm and fascination of the Border.

Perhaps the gentleman named Mr. Ramsay summed them up best when he wrote that their ancestry included a lion, a frog, a hedgehog and a monkey!

The Border is a rather undemonstrative dog, a shade dour, but no less devoted to its owner for that. It does not gush, enthuse or grovel as do some other breeds, but by the occasional meaning glance or by its close presence, it will indicate that it is with you all the way. I feel that one enters into a working partnership with a Border, rather than owning it. They respect and love their owner but are a brainy breed which will work things out for themselves; consequently there is a degree of independence of mind, which must be understood and respected by the owner. This is not rank disobedience but if not convenient to human plans, the Border must be gently persuaded to conform or compromise.

The breed has great dignity and self respect and the Border likes to retain this dignity at all times. In extreme pain or fear it will not show this by screaming but by a general stiffening and the straight ahead stare, so typical of the breed. It always amuses me when I take my Borders to have their inoculations and boosters and am holding them, that they always adopt this attitude and never wince or move. When the needle enters they just stare straight past me and the veterinary surgeon in a "turned-off" manner. This does make it very difficult to locate the source of pain on an injured Border, as it would be "infra dig" for the victim to move a muscle or bat the proverbial eyelid when one reaches the agonizing spot!

To scold a Border who has done wrong is perfectly adequate punishment. This will injure its pride and cause a hurt as deep lasting as physical violence. This is not a breed to take a beating, the bond of trust and mutual respect would be severed for ever. My own dogs have been known to go for days without acknowledging my presence following a scolding—at the end of which time I have felt full of remorse for so offending them! I have known a dog which I had owned for many years, but which had previously had several homes, disappear under the nearest chair or bench at a show in a state of trembling terror when one of its previous owners appeared at the ringside, who had obviously been very hard on her. I used to dread seeing this person at a show, he seemed such a nice man, but my usually happy Border told me otherwise, even though this had occurred several years previously.

They are a most versatile and adaptable breed which seem equally at home living a hard working terrier's life or leading the rather cushy life of a house-pet. In the latter vocation, their figures need watching, as they become fat on very little, and constant scraps and snacks soon pile the weight onto their backs.

Originally bred to bolt foxes in the Northumbrian border districts, with mounted foxhound packs, they are active and game working terriers. They make excellent terriers to otter and badger, as well as fox, and overseas readily work the indigenous animals of their countries of adoption. They are slower to "enter" than some of the other more gassy breeds of working terrier, but once entered generally make a very steady, reliable terrier, very game with a strong streak of commonsense. Some, usually those who are entered too young, may become rather too hard, but generally they are cool-headed. They also make excellent ratters.

They make excellent housedogs, being a very handy size and requiring very little space, and are unobtrusive and sensible. They do not crave attention from their owner at all times by constant nudging and encroachment. I find my dogs enjoy a "love-in" about once a day, otherwise the odd encouraging word suffices. There is a certain amount of moulting throughout the year and the coat usually needs stripping right out twice a year. Their own habits are fastidiously clean—there are of course exceptions to every rule. Their feet are neat, so that there are no unduly large muddy footprints to contend with. They are not generally a very noisy breed, although some will comment vocally with a sort of yodel when pleased. I have known several to grin with their facial expression, eyes and ears.

One I knew who could not hear any sort of music without joining in, with the most melodious series of howls— much to the fury of his rather musical family. It was most entertaining to watch him trying to restrain himself when they told him not to do this, the music just had to come bursting out. Most kennel Borders will have a good sing several times a day. This I think is a characteristic acquired from many generations living in hunt kennels, as this is a habit of hounds. Even Border puppies in the nest will throw back their heads and have a good sing, tails always wagging. The angel choir we call it.

As a first dog for a young boy of ten or eleven years old, I can think of no better breed. They are devoted pals, game for anything, be it ratting around the henhouses or along the river banks, learning tricks, following his pony, sitting beside him while he daydreams, or even working as a beater for him shooting. I have known very many Borders fulfil this important post of first dog with tremendous success.

Every Border seems to have an inborn game sense, no doubt tracing back to the rather dubious way of life of some of the earliest breeders, who probably used them to fill the stew pot as well as to keep the foxes under control. They make excellent beaters, having very good noses, but the real danger is their colour, and I regret to say that several have met their end from trigger-happy guns. They can be taught to retrieve quite easily, and have surprisingly soft mouths, but will usually kill anything that is alive. My Barn Owl is an expert at picking a rabbit or leveret out of a seat, which she then dispatches, and retrieves to me (self-taught), straight to hand and with the speed and style of a trial gundog. However she, like several others that I know, is extremely gunshy; I think she may have very sensitive hearing as well as a very well developed nose. Although they associate the gun with work, they never get over gunshyness, in fact it gets worse rather than better. Of course, this is not the work for which they were bred, and I always explain this to those who think they should make perfect gundogs.

Having good noses, they make splendid tracking dogs. I believe that this sport is pursued with them in Sweden. I have laid lines for them myself with a dead stoat or rat and they really can hunt well. It is interesting to note that in the last war they were specifically advertised for as war dogs, and although I do not know for what purpose they were required, I imagine that it might have been for tracking. At one time terrier trails were run in Yorkshire, on the same lines as hound trails, but these seemed to have died out now, perhaps the contestants could not resist diversions en route in the form of ground game and holes!

Commands are easily taught, but to show independence, are not instantly obeyed. "Message received—over and out" is the Border's response to a command. Then, to

8

show willing, it will do what it thinks will make an adequate compromise of obeyance. For instance, "sit" does not mean an instant clapping of the rear-end to the ground, but the Border will obey by standing rock still where it is, until told to move. There are several dedicated persons who train Borders to high standards for Obedience qualifications. They have my full admiration for their skill and patience.

The Border likes to be the right side of the Law and to keep out of trouble whenever possible. They are not aggressive like some other terriers but once challenged will fight until the death if necessary, and will bear a grudge for ever against their aggressor. The great thing is never to allow the circumstances to occur which might start a fight. Great care should be taken when re-introducing a terrier to the "pack" who has been out working, showing, for stud purposes, having a litter, or even spending an afternoon in the car with you. I started two of my Champion bitches fighting, who had lived together happily and been the greatest of friends, by a careless mistake when re-introducing them after one had been away to be mated. They could never be trusted together after that although they would work together with safety, as they were then thinking of their quarry, the fox, instead of each other.

Borders are usually very good with children, long-suffering and patient. However, as with any other dog, children should not be allowed to take liberties by tormenting or hurting them, neither should unnecessary risks be taken, such as leaving a Border alone in a car with a baby who might start to cry. In these circumstances, any dog might well become frantic. Neither should any child ever be allowed to interfere with a dog that is eating, EVER.

There is however, one snag to the breed, with children and adults. Some Borders will demonstrate affection, understanding or even humour, by leaping up and giving a quick, gentle, nip on the arm or wrist. Although this

9

is well meant, it could terrify a child. Also, sometimes when a child dashes past, I have known Borders take a quick grab at the arm, from excitement I think. These habits I have found impossible to cure, and have found they may come in any strain. Another time that they may do this is when you leave them at bedtime or after having had a chat and a stroke with them. When they play with each other, they give these little nips, I have noticed.

One of my funniest experiences was one lovely lazy afternoon, I was sitting watching my Borders play their usual game of mock fighting, and I realized that I had picked up a word of dog language. To click one's teeth in a certain way meant "let's play". Next time one of the Borders dropped out of the game to speak to me I made the appropriate noise. It stopped dead in its tracks, staring at me with utter disbelief, and then went quite crazy, tearing around me and including me in the game. Another word of Border language that I understand is that, having been offered food or drink, a little lick on the wrist means "no thank you".

With livestock they can be taught to be trustworthy. Like any dog, they will all try their luck with sheep, and have to be reprimanded for this. Once mine have learnt this sharp lesson, there is for ever afterwards a "look at me not chasing sheep" air about them, one even going so far as to brush against my legs every time she saw sheep to make sure that I had noticed!

If brought up young enough with cats, they will live happily with them. However a great many are devils with cats—some are one hundred per cent with their own cats, but lethal to others. With young chickens there is a certain unswerving determination. I have found that however much one drums in "no", sooner or later the opportunity arises, and the Border will sneak off and "do" them. I have known them wait weeks for the occasion to be right, and then that is that.

Apart from very young puppies, they are not a car sick breed, and usually love to travel in the car. Mine often spend several nights away from home in the car which seems to be a huge treat—a change being as good as a cure.

When furious, with dignity hurt, the Border will turn its back on you in such a very stolid, prickly way, that there is no doubt whatsoever of its meaning; a furious Border looks very hedgehog-like with head down, coat sticking out, posterior tucked under. I remember one rather elderly, tub-like Border coming for a walk, supposedly a treat for her, with my mother's Labradors. These considered it a great game to gallop straight over Nellie, felling her to the ground every time, and pretending they had not seen her. She became more and more hedgehog-like, and instead of seeing them off with one snap, she persisted in stumping in a straight line down the moor, picking herself up each time she was bowled over, putting her head down, and setting off again, pretending they weren't there. Being a typical Border she was not going to protest out loud at such uncouth behaviour.

One of my favourite Borders was a devil for cats, a killer. She used to travel to shows sitting on my knee in the front of the car (I was not driving in those days I hasten to add). If a cat was in sight she used to lurch forward automatically to try to get it. Of course, we could not resist shouting "there's a cat" whenever we saw one and she reacted every time. One day, on a particularly tedious car journey, my mother and I became involved in a religious discussion—to our amazement 'Pep' kept leaping forward at the window when there was nothing feline in view—eventually we discovered this was every time we mentioned the words "Roman Catholic"—we had to hastily change the conversation to a more mundane topic.

In the following chapter I shall try to describe the physical attributes of the Border Terrier, having roughly detailed the character of the breed in this one. The last chapter contains several anecdotes illustrating some of their characteristics of gameness, pluck and determination.

11

CHAPTER 2

The Breed Standard and Its Interpretation

The Kennel Club Standard. Border Terrier

Characteristics.—The Border Terrier is essentially a working Terrier. It should be able to follow a horse and must combine activity with gameness.

Head and Skull.—Head like that of an otter, moderately broad in skull with a short strong muzzle; a black nose is preferable but a liver or flesh-coloured one is not a serious fault.

Eyes.—Dark, with keen expression.

Ears.—Small, V-shaped, of moderate thickness and dropping forward close to the cheek.

Mouth.—Teeth should have a scissor-like grip, with the top teeth slightly in front of the lower, but level mouth is quite acceptable. An undershot or overshot mouth is a major fault and highly undesirable.

Neck.—Of moderate length.

Forequarters.—Forelegs straight and not too heavy in bone.

Body.—Deep and narrow and fairly long; ribs carried well back, but not oversprung, as a terrier should be capable of being spanned by both hands behind the shoulder.

Hindquarters.—Racy. Loin strong.

Feet.—Small with thick pads.

Tail.—Moderately short and fairly thick at the base, then tapering, set high and carried gaily but not curled over the back.

Coat.—Harsh and dense with close undercoat. The skin must be thick.

Colour.—Red, wheaten, grizzle and tan or blue and tan.

Weight and size.—Weight: Dogs, between 13–15½ lbs.; Bitches, between 11½–14 lbs.

NOTE:—Male animals should have two apparently normal testicles fully descended into the scrotum.

(reproduced by kind permission of the Kennel Club.)

The Standard was laid down to describe the ideal Border for the work for which the breed was bred for very many years before it gained official recognition. This is the blueprint for producing the type of terrier to follow a horse and to work foxes in Northumberland.

The first paragraph emphasises that the breed is essentially a working terrier, and must be of active build with total freedom of movement and the gameness to do its job effectively. We can assume that stamina is also required.

The head is probably the outstanding feature of the breed, most people realizing that their heads are different to those of any other terrier. The words "moderately broad in skull" should be noted and these should prevent the head becoming grotesquely broad as an exaggerated show point. If one studies an otter head it will be observed that there is no exaggeration anywhere, in fact it is a rather refined head. As the Standard says "head like that of an otter" I take this to mean the whole head, not just the skull, to be otterlike. The head of an otter is designed to lie flat on the surface of the water when the animal swims; this means a flat, shallow head, rather like an old-fashioned tobacco pouch in shape. Tremendous depth from occiput to jaw is not otterlike, more Griffon-like. The muzzle should be short and strong, and I expect the jaw to be strong too. The proportions of an otter head are $\frac{2}{3}$ from occiput to stop, and $\frac{1}{3}$ from stop to nose-tip. An otter does not have a pronounced stop, but there is a definite suggestion of one. When studying different otters, one soon realizes that these vary tremendously in their heads as individuals. Recently I studied two in a Wild Life Park, one of which was a

13

fine English dog otter with a head which would look good on a Border, the other was a different species with a horrid little head which I should have penalized had it been shown under me! It was very gratifying to hear a young boy, a member of the general public, who was going around the benches at a show, say, after staring long and hard at one of my dogs, "I could breed otters from that one." Not so pleasing was the know-all who under similar conditions, said to her friend "that one has the typical badger face"!

Eyes should be dark in colour, and not too prominent as they present themselves for injury working if they are. They should not be placed too close together—this nearly always denotes a "terrier" head, not a true Border head, nor so wide apart as to remind one of a Staffordshire Bull Terrier. A very wise maxim is that if you think the dog's expression is wrong you can take it that the eye is set wrong in the skull, and therefore the whole of the dog's head is wrong. A similar edict, wise and true, which applies to every part of any breed of dog, is that if you are worried whether something is not quite right, you can take it that it is wrong, as it would not strike your eye as peculiar were it right.

The ears must drop forward close to the cheek. They must not be set on too high, should never break above the line of the skull and should not lie fox-terrier-like above the eye. Neither should they fly, that is stick out sideways from the skull. A teething puppy must be forgiven flying ears, as the ear-carriage becomes very erratic at this stage of development. Rounded and pendulous ears are incorrect, and terribly hereditary, appearing for generations despite careful efforts being made to breed them out. The Standard does not call for the ear to be dark, but a dark V-shaped ear definitely sets off the head and expression to best advantage. A brown ear, as a liver nose, should not be penalized as this is entirely personal fancy.

The teeth should be in a normal scissorlike bite, the

top ones slightly overlapping the lower ones when the mouth is viewed from the side. Full dentition is of course required, with forty-two large, strong and even teeth. The bite of a Border does alter with age. No-one seems able to account for this but it has been suggested that the jaws grow throughout the life of the dog or that the bones of the face alter slightly with age. Certainly the jaws of young puppies seem to grow at different rates. A level-bite is one where the teeth meet together tip-to-tip instead of overlapping slightly. An undershot bite is where the teeth of the lower jaw overlap those of the top jaw. Judges do not penalize an odd tooth out of line or missing, as this can be caused through a working accident, although of course a correct bite is preferable as the teeth will be less likely to be loosened at work. Once one tooth is loose and falls out, those on either side will shift position slightly and so their moorings will be weakened and they become more prone to damage. On no account should a Border with an undershot mouth be bred from. A mouth often encountered in the breed is that where a couple of teeth are out of line on one side, one tooth may be undershot, and the others correct. This mouth is sometimes accepted by judges, but it must be remembered that it is not a correct mouth, and is geneticaly a wrong mouth. This is another difficult fault to breed out; it reproduces itself exactly for generations. As the dog grows older, more teeth come forward until the whole mouth becomes undershot. These teeth wear badly too, being uneven, and such a dog will have stumps instead of teeth in it's declining years. One thing is certain about mouths, bad ones never improve, although good ones may become worse.

The neck should be long enough to allow freedom of head movement, and fairly strong as the dog may have to draw a dead fox with it's teeth.

For galloping, a well laid, clean shoulder, with a long upper arm is required. The forelegs must be straight with sound bone, neither too heavy nor too light. Spindly or brittle bone would be unservicable for the jumping up and down amongst rocks and over walls that a Border must do, resulting in broken legs. The elbows should be perfectly free, neither tied-in nor loose. Tied-in elbows are best described by the dog appearing to be wearing a tight elastic band around the elbows: the front movement is badly affected, the front feet being twisted to the side instead of moving straight forward. This fault in construction really does hamper a working dog, as the effort to walk wears them out and they cannot travel across country with ease. One never sees this fault on pack hounds. Another very irritating aspect of tied-in elbows on a working terrier is that it makes it quite impossible to "post" the terrier down a small hole, as the front-legs form a V against the side of the hole, the feet being wider apart than the legs at the elbow.

The body is another very characteristic point, being that of a galloping dog. There must be heart-room so the dog should not be slab-sided, but the ribs should not be over-sprung. A short-coupled Border is contrary to the standard, the length being essential for the terrier to turn around in a small hole. The ribs should be carried well back. The Border should be able to be spanned by a normal man's hands, just behind the shoulder; it should also come up in one hand perfectly balanced, the hand being placed just under the brisket. This enables the terrier to be passed around when working.

The hindquarters are those of a galloping dog. They are not described in great detail; my own interpretation is that there should be a long, slightly sloping pelvis, long well bent stifles—but not over-bent, neat, low-set hocks at a right-angle to the ground, the hindquarters being free and capable of standing out behind the perpendicular line dropped from the root of the tail, with well developed long thigh and second thigh muscles, and the hocks turning neither in nor out. The loin should be strong and muscular, possibly slightly arched.

Movement should be absolutely free, straight and true, the dog travelling forward with an effortless economy of motion. The forelegs should swing straight through from the shoulders, with a forward reaching low movement. One should not be aware of twisting wrists and swinging feet, the knees or the elbows. The propulsion of the dog comes from the rear; the dog should move forward with tremendous drive from the hocks, the hind leg reaching well forward under the dog and pushing out behind the dog. No wasted effort should be made. Bicycling action or whirring hind legs do not progress forward, but upwards. The dog should move forwards all the time, covering the ground well in action.

Viewed from the front, the forelegs should be parallel in motion, no twisting wrists and feet; from the rear, the hocks should be neither so wide apart as to cause the dog to straddle, nor so close together that the thighs rub together, and they should turn neither in nor out. The dog should stand and move evenly on all the pads; worn pads or uneven length of toenails denote a fault in movement.

Feet must be small, the pads thick and neat and dark. The feet in the breed have improved greatly since I first entered the ring and one scarcely ever encounters the long hare-feet with thin, pink pads and light toenails. The feet must stand up to work and are a very vital point on the terrier—the terrier at home on three legs being very little use when a fox is run to ground.

The tail is another breed characteristic, being carrot-like in shape and never docked. This is the handle by which the dog is pulled out of a hole working. It should be set on high, but not as high as a Fox Terrier as this does not make sense with the longer back of the Border, and is carried gaily, but not curled over the back. Very often the Border will drop it when standing in the show-ring. This should not be penalized as it is typical of the breed character.

17

Coat is most important, and should be as described in the Standard. For show the dog should be presented with undercoat left in. Over-tidying spoils the general appearance and character as the "tweedy" look is lost, besides which the full coat is required for work—and the judges are supposed to judge to the Standard which describes a working dog. The skin, or pelt, is another important point; this should be loose-fitting and thick. The terrier in a tight place can manouevre himself along inside it, rather on the same principle as the design of a caterpillar tractor.

Colour is immaterial. The specified colours are all correct, and all as correct as each other. Working terrier men claim that red is too fox-like in colour, but even a white terrier is earth coloured when it has been to ground. A little white on the chest does not matter, but white toes do not meet with much approval.

The weights given may be on the light side, but should serve as a reminder that the lighter weight terriers are better and should be aimed for, bearing in mind that dogs are probably better fed and reared now than in the days when the Standard was drawn up. Any suggested alteration to the weight should be opposed, as this would mean that the correctly sized dogs would be penalized and the breed would become bigger and bigger. As a rough guide the old working terrier man's maxim of an inch per pound serves as a guide as to height.

There is a slight incidence of monorchidism (one testicle descended) and cryptorchidism (no testicles descended) in the breed. However, if breeders pay due regard to this in their breeding plans this should not become a major problem. This is a hereditary fault, and a serious one, so monorchids should on no account be bred from.

The points system which one sees published in various Border Terrier publications is an anachronism and should be ignored. The Kennel Club deleted this from the Standard many years ago, it having been proved that no points system of judging livestock works, the overall balanced and unexaggerated animal being the ideal.

Although the Standard has been criticised for leaving too much to the imagination, I maintain that if one knows the job of a working terrier, and has taken the trouble to find out from a good source the basic anatomy of a dog, the Standard puts the finishing stitches to the tapestry of the Border.

Type cannot be laid down in any Standard and is impossible to define as it is a personal interpretation of what one sees. It is true to say that if the dog reminds you of any other breed of dog it fails in type. The most common alien types one may spot in Borders are those bearing a resemblance to Griffons Bruxellois, Working Collies, Staffordshire Bull Terriers, Irish Terriers, Cairn Terriers and Whippets. I know exactly what is, to my eye, a typical Border, but this I cannot describe to anyone else except by pointing to individual dogs to illustrate this. Type is stamped all over the dog, not just the head. Too long and straight pasterns denote Irish Terrier type, a slack backline and tail pointing to the ground denote Sheepdog.

Kennel type differs again, and well established strains will develop their own type within the Breed type. Unfortunately we do not have many kennels breeding a true strain; this is a most useful thing to have in a breed, as should disaster occur in one strain, breeders can turn to another line, instead of the whole of the breeders following the same pattern of breeding. In my experience the kennels which have produced a distinct kennel type, which would enable one to pinpoint the strain should one meet a Border in Paris or San Francisco, have been or are, the F.F. strain of the Forster family, Mr. Renton's strain, the Portholme, Deerstone, Wharfholm, Maxton, Dandyhow, Eignwye, Foxhill and Hawkesburn kennels. Others may have produced dogs similar to each other in construction, but not of such distinct type.

Mr. Hugh Pybus said that he remembered the breed at the end of the last Century. There were then two distinct types, those from the North Tyne district, which were in outline like the present day Border, but lighter boned and with a longer head, and those from the Wandbeck and Coquet districts, which were smaller, with shorter faces and with a "topin" of light soft hair on the head. He did not remember what the Redesdale and Catcleugh type was like. These distinctive types could well account for the fact that Border litters are often very uneven with a great variation in type amongst members of the same litter.

In the past there was a noticeable difference in type between the Borders in the north and those in the south of England, the latter being stockier in build and shorter on the leg. However, this has now been completely erradicated by judicious breeders in the south using northern dogs, and vice versa, all to the betterment of the breed.

Type and soundness are both important in the make-up of a good Border, coupled with true Breed character. Everyone strives to produce their own ideal Border, but we all suffer the same set backs and disappointments, losing on the swings what we gain on the roundabouts, which is what makes dog breeding such an enthralling past-time. By breeding and judging to the Standard the breed should retain the ability to work fearlessly, to be a good-looking dog, and an ideal companion.

CHAPTER 3

Working

The Terrier Song

Now there's many a song about hunting,
Packs and huntsmen are honoured by name,
But there isn't a song about terriers
Which in Lakeland have gained lasting fame.

Chorus:

So always remember your terriers,
Protect them from wet and from cold,
For the love of a tyke for his master
Can never be measured in gold.

Whether it's Fury or Trixie or Nellie,
Or Rock, Jock or Turk it's the same,
One quality you'll find among them,
And dalesfolk call it "dead game".
And whether he's rough or smooth-coated,
He'll tackle badger, otter or fox,
Run a drain or creep into a soil-hole,
Or squeeze through a grike in the rocks.

Chorus:

He'll yield not one inch though they maul him,
He'll fight to the death on his own,
Though sometimes he'll be imprisoned
By a rush-in of soil or of stone.
And then the brave lads of the valleys
To save him will toil day and night,
And join in a Hallo of triumph
As he blinks back to God's blessed light.

Chorus:

Now at Cruft's famous show down in London,
They have Lakelands that aren't worth the name.
If you showed 'em a fox or an otter
They fly for their lives without shame.
They're not built to creep or do battle,
But to sit on a chair in a house,
And they do say that one recent champion
Was chased down the road by a mouse!

Chorus:

So here's to our gallant laal workers,
Not beauties, perhaps, but they'll do.
With gameness they've also affection,
And make you a pal good and true.
And when your terrier, in old age, is dying,
And the world all around you seems sad,
A lick on the hand will console you,
For a truer friend man never had.

Final Chorus:

Sung to the tune "Laal Melbreak".
(reproduced by kind permission of the author, Mr. D. P. Todd, Kendal)

NOTE: Although written primarily with the Lakeland Terrier in mind, the sentiment contained in this song applies equally to the Border Terrier.
A.R-W.

A very versatile working terrier by adoption, the Border was originally bred to work with the mounted packs of foxhounds on the hilly parts of north Northumberland. This entailed following the hunt cross-country, and when the fox was eventually run to ground the Border was required to bolt it, if possible, or otherwise to kill and draw it. It is for these requirements that the blueprint of the breed as laid down in the Standard was formulated.

The term "work" as applied to a Border means working to fox with hounds primarily, or to otter with hounds —and by general acceptance of the term in this day and age, although not strictly correct, working either fox, otter or badger. Although the breed make adept ratters, gun-dogs, tracking experts and some have even gained obedience qualifications, none of these past-times should be called "work".

Borders are considerably slower to enter than other more fiery breeds of working terrier, and for this reason are sometimes misunderstood and termed useless too early in life. As a rule they do make steady and reliable terriers, although sometimes those that are entered too early become too hard in later life.

The temptation to do too much too early with a young terrier should be avoided. A Border should not be put to fox, otter or badger before it is well over twelve months old. However, there is a great deal of homework that can be done with a youngster up to this age, which will help towards the great moment when it gets it's first chance to "go", later on. It is no use arriving panting at an earth with a teenage terrier who knows "nowt", and expect to be able to push it to ground with the toe of one's boot!

Once a puppy has fully changed its teeth, it may start learning to worry an old sock or rag attached firmly to a strong piece of string. Nylon materials should not be used for worrying as it can damage the teeth, having no "give" in it. This worrying will awaken the latent sporting instincts—if not already awoken by poultry, cats, sheep and other temptations. The rag is trailed around a little on the ground, with realistic twitching movements, until the interest of the puppy has been caught. Once the puppy tries to creep up on the rag to investigate it, the string is allowed to slacken so that the rag is still whilst the pup creeps up. As the pup stretches out to sniff the rag the string is twitched—the pup will dart back—but, by slackening the string again, the pup will soon approach again. By moving the rag a little more each time the pup will soon be persuaded to chase it and pounce at it, and by speeding up the movement the pup will soon be flying around and should be allowed to

23

catch it before he gets bored with the game. Now the string is pulled taut, and with the pup hanging on, the rag is pulled around. Should the pup loose it's grip the process is repeated until the pup is shaking and killing the rag. The string is now loosened while the pup worries the rag but, as soon as it leaves go or changes it's grip, the rag is jerked around which will inspire the pup to kill it dead next time. Once the pup is totally engrossed in this game, encouraging noises are made but if these appear to put the pup off they should cease and be renewed quietly once it is worrying again. As in any form of training, this lesson should be brief and cease while the pup is still fascinated and wanting more.

The next step is to put the rag somewhere the puppy will have to go either into or under, such as a dog kennel or henhouse—not too far in at first so that the pup can reach it's neck and shoulders in to grab the rag—and then further under so that the pup has to crawl in to get it out. By holding the string and jerking at the right time, the youngster can be made to believe that the object is alive and needs killing. When the pup is "killing", I make realistic squeaking noises and the universal language of terrier men and terriers, the prolonged hissing, which being translated means "get in and get 'im".

If one can procure a piece of foxskin (straight off a fox, not cured!) or even better, a brush, this is substituted for the rag as it is of course more realistic and has that delicious aroma which a terrier must learn to detect.

No opportunity to procure a corpse should be overlooked as so much can be done to educate a terrier with a dead stoat, fox or similar mammal. In my better days, when I was a little darling of around nine years old, I attended a Field Trial in East Yorkshire, wearing my best school macintosh. During the course of the day a stoat ran down the line of guns and on the instruction of the gamekeeper was shot. The delightful child made a lasting impression in the district by asking the favour of the corpse, and carrying it all day in her pocket. I still cannot show my face in that area without being reminded of the incident.

Those gundog people may have mocked but how useful that stoat proved. Attached to a long cord, it was trailed through the woods at Lilymere and finally, with the aid of a long forked stick, went to ground up the artificial drain. The whole terrier pack was then laid on the line which the youngsters soon learnt how to hunt and then they all shot up the drain whereupon my brother, who by now had the end of the string in his hand, pulled the stoat out and a good worry was had of the corpse, amidst whoops and holloas. Later that day the youngsters had their turn up the drain, and again the next day. For obvious reasons I would not advocate using a corpse much after the third day—how Burke and Hare this all sounds!

From this the youngster progresses to rats. Should one have rats around fodder bins, by leaving the lid of one of these bins open when the level of food is low in the bin, one can create the ideal opportunity for a youngster to meet his first rat, there often being a couple of young rats at the bottom of the bin in the morning. In modern times of Men From The Ministry and Inspectors rats are frowned upon—but, luckily for terriers, rats will be rats and take little notice of legislation passed against them in Westminster.

Here I must emphasise that whatever one is doing with working terriers the quarry should be treated as humanely as possible and despatched as quickly as possible—and that a rat should be treated with as much consideration as an otter and should never be tormented or allowed to suffer. An experienced terrier is as humane a method of despatching rats as any that I know.

Back to the rats in the bin. Half grown rats are the best to start a youngster as the mommas and poppas can take some handling and can give a nasty bite if not despatched immediately. These should be left for an experienced terrier who will kill them instantly with one shake. The young terrier may not like being dropped into a dark bin but the lid must be quickly replaced otherwise the rats will use the terrier as a ladder to freedom. Once the rat moves the pup will get the idea, but should it not shape, drop in a more experienced terrier to join it. They soon learn.

Terriers soon learn from each other the art of ratting around farmyards and buildings and along river banks, and become amazingly sharp at picking up rats.

A great deal of terrier lore can be passed down from an experienced terrier to a youngster by example. Once one has a pack of terriers without an entered terrier amongst them it is much more difficult to enter them. A trustworthy terrier is invaluable as the owner will be able to use it to see whether or not the youngsters are telling the truth when they say a drain is uninhabited or otherwise, and also what the quarry is, an essential item of information when working young and inexperienced terriers.

An artificial drain is most useful, and easily made. In it's simplest form this in an L-shaped trench, with a covered top. The terrier goes in at the end of the long arm of the L, and at the end of the short arm there is a removable covering, so that the terrier can run through the drain. The entrance should be terrier-sized, not too gaping, so that the dog becomes accustomed to squeezing into a hole which touches on all sides. With the aid of the rag, or body, the terrier learns to go further and further up the drain—or it will learn this by following another terrier. Drains under lanes and cart-tracks and tree roots are useful for practising a terrier but do beware of traps set in them in unknown territory. Also, a youngster should not be put into a place where there may be a badger.

It is more difficult to find work for terriers than gundogs as one cannot take the terrier work in a district as one can a shoot. The local hunt will make it's own arrangements for terrier work but if one appears frequently, behaves properly, and keeps one's terriers on a lead at all times, and they are quiet and not aggressive, the opportunity may present itself. One must try to make a point of being the first there when the fox is run to ground; one day the hunt terriers will not have arrived and the great moment will come. This may be a place that the huntsman considers suitable for a follower to try their terrier. Now is the time that the terrier must go straight to ground, and all the messing around under cart-tracks and in artificial drains will be worthwhile. A youngster is best sent in to follow an experienced terrier for the first time. It will nearly always follow the other terrier and the older terrier can show him by demonstration what to do when confronted by Reynard, how to use his voice, and how to find his way out through complex side drains without getting lost.

Once one's terriers are discovered to be useful and game, more and more opportunity for working them will present itself and they will gain experience.

Should the hunt not be helpful in respect of offering work to outside terriers, a few words around the grapevine that there are some terriers willing to have a try usually produces results. A word to the local gamekeeper will not come amiss. There are a great number of people working terriers in various ways, up and down the country, and with tact and patience it is possible to join them.

Here I should mention that one cannot just go anywhere and work terriers. All land is owned by someone, and this particular someone may like their foxes, otters and badgers to remain undisturbed. Most land is hunted over, and the local hunt does not like interference in their district. Also, of course, this is trespassing. Badgers are now protected by law, and may not be dug except within the terms of the law.

The term "entered" terrier, as applied to working, means one that has been to either fox, otter or badger,

27

and become thoroughly experienced with that quarry—going to ground and staying with that quarry until either dug down to from above, or the quarry has bolted, or the terrier is called out by it's owner. It should bay it's quarry: a silent terrier telling those above nothing about it's whereabouts, or quarry. One could say that an entered terrier has the equivalent of a M.A. or other degree, having studied its subject in depth.

Every time a terrier goes to ground, there is a risk that it may meet with an accident. Therefore this risk should be fully appreciated before working a terrier, and on no account should terriers be allowed to roam off around earths by themselves. Once they have discovered the local earth, this becomes a real hazard, and my advice is NEVER to show them where it is, however tempting to let them have a go under supervision.

Loss of life occurs through a variety of reasons, such as a fall of light earth or sand in which case the dog suffocates, dropping down to a level from which the dog cannot jump up again, becoming trapped between two dead animals, being badly injured, taking a wrong turning in one of catacomb-like ramifications which one meets in limestone country, and so on.

Another ever-present risk is that of being worried by hounds. This is nearly always the fault of the human element becoming over excited, and halloaing the bolting quarry before the terrier, which usually follows close on it's heels, has been picked up. When this happens it is very distressing for everyone, so all care should be taken for the terrier to be picked up immediately it surfaces from the earth. Whatever the colour of the terrier before going to ground, it will emerge the same colour as the earth, sometimes wet and muddy, and smelling of fox or otter.

Care should also be taken to see that no more than two, or at the very most, three terriers are put to ground together. Should too many go in at once, those at the rear will press forward, and those at the front will be pushed too close for comfort to the quarry, and, being unable to back away, will receive heavy punishment.

It is quite amazing the amount of punishment a Border will take, and equally amazing the speed with which even the most ghastly bites will heal. However, a badly bitten terrier should be kept at home until healed although the "patient" will disagree with you, come hunting mornings. I am a great believer in disinfecting all bites—they are sore anyway—so I am fairly free with the disinfectant. This applies to all bites, but especially to rat-bites. A tube of anti-septic ointment with a long nozzle to put into deep wounds should be part of every working terrier man's equipment, and should be kept in stock at all times.

Should a terrier be lost underground, help will be forthcoming from many and varied sources. This is the worst fate of all, both for terrier and the owner, who will spend many sleepless nights until the terrier is accounted for, one way or the other. There is an excellent club formed expressly for the purpose of rescuing trapped terriers which has all the right equipment for rock-moving and blasting, and hundreds of willing helpers. The Fell and Moorland Working Terrier Club is the most laudable organization and anyone intending to work terriers would be well advised to become a member, and to find the telephone number of the nearest representative of the club—just in case.

I maintain that battle-scars are not necessarily credit-able—they may denote a fool and my immediate answer when proudly shown these wounds is to think—and—more often than not say—"let's hope he has more sense next time". One cannot judge the prowess of a working terrier by any outside visible signs—only when he is at his vocation. Some Borders do become too hard: to quote Jack Price "if you've got a good 'un in a Border it isn't a good'un, it's too hard". This may be true in some strains, but by and large they are sensible, courag-eous and steady terriers.

My father's Borders, Smuts and Squill, were two of the best terriers one could wish for. Extremely reliable, full of pluck, they worked between them a total of some eighteen seasons to otter, fox and badger. Smuts, although he has been dead for some fifteen years, is still talked about frequently and remembered as a "king-dog", a perfect gentleman and a fearless warrior, affectionately known as "the General" by us.

He was given to my father as being a villainous puppy, but never did anything wrong throughout his thirteen years with us. A very good-looking dog but with the worst coat I have yet seen on a Border, scissored all over by my mother, he won Best of Breed at Kendal show under Jimmy Garrow—to this day that is remembered but luckily the owner was forgotten and it is talked about as "that good Border that was scissored all over", I look very innocent meanwhile! Marked-up only once, except during the "Saga of Smuts" which follows, no-one seeing this dog in the showring could tell his working ability—no "fire" here, his head and tail drooped, no scars, and the worst non-weatherproof coat ever—but I bet there was no gamer or more experienced dog in the ring! He took to, or rather, I made him attend, Championship shows at the age of ten, and how proud I am still of the first first prize which I ever won at a Championship show, with him in the Working class at Carlisle under Mr. Hancock, and of his veteran shield won at the Yorkshire, Lancashire and Cheshire show.

Smuts was extremely lucky to reach old age at all, as in the winter of 1954 he and Squill were put to ground in an innocent-looking borran on Leck Fell, whilst hunting with the Lunesdale Foxhounds. Squill eventually emerged, but not so Smuts, who had to be left there for the night. The entrance to the hole was blocked with rocks, after a bed of straw had been left, with some food, inside, so that should he come out he would curl up there and wait for collection in the morning, instead of wandering over the fells and becoming lost. The weather was of the worst February sort with hard frost and deep snow. However, Smuts was not on his bed in the morning, and although all efforts were made to rescue him, it proved impossible to dig on account of the limestone rocks. The army was consulted, after a few sleepless nights and anxious days, to see whether the hole could be blasted, but that would prove too dangerous. By this time the weather had worsened, and it became impossible to get out of the drive at Lilymere to visit the hole. However, Mr. Arthur Swettenham, the local gamekeeper, walked up the fell faithfully every day to visit the hole, and on the eleventh morning, there was a scarcely-recognisable Smuts lying on the straw. His injuries were terrible, a broken nose-bone, blind in one eye, as well as being de-hydrated and very thin. However, with expert attention from the Veterinary Surgeon who had been standing-by all this time in the surgery to receive him, should he be alive, and careful nursing he recovered. Although he had to take several months leave for convalescence, once fully recovered he resumed his work with all the pluck as before, and although his sight was very poor, it was quite remarkable how he could spot an otter venting on the surface of the water.

Another of my treasured possessions is an otter mask, mounted, and inscribed "K.D.O.H. Otterpot May 16 1951 bolted twice Smuts". The story of this being that Smuts was put into a rather difficult tree-root to bolt an otter which he did, after some hard work to persuade it to leave. The crowd spectating on the bank opposite the root could not contain their excitement, and holloaed before Smuts had been picked up and put on his lead. Hounds came tearing to the spot as Smuts emerged, and he disappeared beneath the stampede. We dreaded what we should find, but he had not been worried, merely trampled into the wet sand, and was obviously in a state of shock. He was put on his lead and watched the rest of the hunt. The otter then went to ground again, and every other terrier was tried in turn, Smuts not being invited as he was on the sick list. All the others failed to make anything of the root, so eventually the willing Smuts was tried again, and with no bother, the otter was bolted. The undoubted hero of that day was Smuts.

Many tales are told of the prowess of Borders in the working field, and very interesting they are too. However, those who claim that their terrier has killed a badger single-handed are looked upon with great suspicion by knowledgable men. It is on record that Titlington Peter owned by Mr. George Sordy, did just that. Peter weighed 15 pounds, and the badger, a healthy one, 26 pounds, so this was indeed no mean feat. He also dragged the dead weight of the badger some eight yards towards the entrance, and that after he had been badly mauled by the badger—a dog of strength, courage and determination. This account was published in Our Dogs at the time.

Working badger is a specialized branch of terrier work, and should not be attempted by "green" terriers—or "green" owners without the help of an expert at the art. Whereas a fox or otter can give a bad bite, a badger can also maul a terrier with its bearlike tallons: these coupled with a self-locking jaw and a very short temper make Brock a fearsome adversary.

Although not the job for which they were bred, Borders make excellent otterhunting terriers. The Dumfries Otterhounds have used them for nearly sixty years, and most other packs have used them from time to time. Tom Harrison, the present huntsman of the Kendal and District pack is a keen Border fan. Charlie Kitchener, who was huntsman and kennel huntsman of this pack in the days of Sir Maurice Bromley-Wilson, had a pack of Borders and near Borders, all of whom answered to the name "Pops"—it being so much easier to have one name for them all, as then he would be sure of having the right terrier when he called "Pops".

A smaller terrier than that used for foxhunting on the Border country comes in handy otterhunting, as otters are very slimly built creatures, being really just an enlarged stoat of the river bank. The Border must have a good double waterproof jacket, built-in agility and stamina, large teeth, and pluck.

Ideally, the terrier should be led until required to work a root or drain, but it is not always easy to find volunteers willing to have their arms tugged out of their sockets all day by two pulling terriers—and believe me, all terriers pull under these circumstances.

Terriers running loose can ruin a good day's hunting. First, when the hounds mark an otter in a drain or tree root, by rushing in the wrong side of the otter, and thus pushing it further back up the drain or root—and making it much more difficult to persuade to leave same. If the terriers are on leads, once hounds have been removed to a reasonable distance, the selected terrier can then be inserted scientifically beyond the otter, which facilitates a speedy exit. Another nuisance loose-running terriers can commit is bolting the otter from a shallow holt too soon into the pack.

If terriers are allowed to run with hounds by habit, they all too easily think they are hounds and will draw the river bank and swim the water for wash instead of going up into the bank. For many years the Kendal had a very handsome, but rather oversize, Border running with them, who made a marvellous mini-Otterhound and proved very useful as such but was never known to go to ground. He would stand back and watch the terrier work with the expert eye of a hound.

Needless to say, it is courting disaster to have otter-headed terriers swimming once there is a hunt away and hounds are looking for the otter's head to surface—anyone who has witnessed a near-disaster of this sort would never take such a risk again.

Whatever the quarry, a terrier must have "voice"—being mute is a bad fault. "Voice" means that when the terrier comes face to face with his opponent he will stand back and bay at him, advancing a little at a time, until the animal can stand it no longer and decides to leave.

An experienced combination of owner and terrier will know exactly what is going on underground, and what the quarry is, by the note of the terrier's voice. By putting one's ear literally to the ground, one can locate the position of the terrier, and listen to the most amazing series of barks, growls, thumps and maybe a yell should the terrier be nipped on the nose, all several feet below the earth.

A good nose is required to locate the quarry, and also to follow the terrier's own line back out of a complicated system of drains, or through the many layers of passages in a badger sett.

A terrier that is aggressive with other dogs is no use whatever for terrier work. He must be able to mingle freely with hounds and other terriers—he may be expected to go to ground with a strange terrier. Should he spar up to hounds, he will sooner or later be picked up and shaken by one. This indeed happened to a bitch of mine who was stupid enough to challenge a stallion hound as he came along the sheeptrod she was standing on, on a steep fellside. He just picked her up and shook her in an absent-minded manner, his mind being on his work. She survived, but through no fault of her own.

Terriers who, when worked up to fever pitch with excitement, fasten on to the nearest thing, are also a menace, as one has not time to separate fighting terriers when there is a fox to ground and dusk is approaching on a fellside.

Strangers will lead, and work, terriers, and will often be left behind at an earth to pick up the terrier should it take some time to emerge. Handshy terriers are not suitable for work. Bad tempered and shy terriers should not be bred, or bred from, and really should be "six-feet under".

The future of terrier work, as we know it, seens uncertain. It is allied to hunting, and various parties are always trying to bar that. All one can do is to enjoy it while one can, and before it becomes an underground sport—no pun intended! As foxes are a real menace to farming communities in certain areas, and remembering that the fell huntsmen were actually recalled from the Second World War such was the need for fox control, let us hope that there will still be a use for our game little terriers for many a long day.

Working Certificates may be given by Masters of Hounds to any terrier who has proved to be a game terrier who will go to ground and stay with it's quarry. These are not easy to gain, simply because one must have the opportunity to demonstrate this ability, and opportunities are hard to come by. It is not possible to enter a promising terrier at a Field Trial, as one can should one have a good gundog. Working certificates need not, contrary to belief, be recorded with a breed club before entering a class at a show for dogs holding these certificates, but evidence of their existence must of course be proved. This is not a Kennel Club award.

There is no doubt that anyone given the equal choice between work and show for Borders, and ever having worked a terrier, would choose work, without any hesitation. There is no thrill like that of seeing your dog doing the work for which it has been bred for generations, using its brains and courage, without help from the owner as once it is down there it is "on it's own". However, if one has a highly prized showdog and would mind the odd tooth knocked out or jaw broken, don't risk it. The choice is yours.

Speaking for myself, I can only say that having carefully prepared my bitch with my sights set on her third C.C. in the morning, and hounds having run through the wood in the afternoon, that bitch was dragged to the fox hole through the most dreadful brambles when the fox was run to ground—"blow her third C.C." I thought —happily to say, she got it, and the next day too!

Nowadays I do not have the time nor opportunity to work my terriers. However, I do as much as I can, and never miss the opportunity to educate them in this field.

Should I ever find that my current show dog is not interested, or has a fault in it's work, I never like that dog again, and it is out on it's ear before you could say "rats". This is with no thought for the benefit of the breed, just for my own satisfaction.

One of my favourite working terrier stories was of the Border who did not emerge from the hole, and, after waiting some time, her irate owner decided to dig to see what was delaying her, only to find her with neck and shoulders firmly wedged through the bottom of an old fashioned chamber pot!

CHAPTER 4

The History of the Border Terrier

Undoubtedly there is a close link between the Border, Bedlington and Dandie Dinmont Terriers, all having originated from the same district, the border between Northumberland and Scotland. Exactly which breed came first appears to have been lost in the mists of antiquity, but the various items of information which we do have piece together to confirm that the Border is an old established breed.

It is generally accepted as true that the Borders, Bedlingtons and Dandie Dinmonts are all descended from terriers bred by the wandering tinkers or muggers who inhabited the locality around the Northumberland border. In later years the terriers were bred by yeoman farmers and shepherds and one can surmise that, as travel from valley to valley would be difficult except on foot over the tops, a slight variation in type would occur in each valley. The Border is said to have originated in Coquetdale; the fact that the Bedlington was known as the Rothbury Terrier, Rothbury being in the Coquet valley, would suggest that these breeds might be inter-related.

The names of two characters known as William Allen, who was born at Bellingham in 1704, and his son James Allen, born at Holystone, who died in 1810, occur in the history of the early Bedlington and Dandie Dinmont, and apparently, the Border Terrier. James Allen, known as "Piper Allen", is described by Sir Walter Scott as "an admirable piper, yet a desperate reprobate . . . . when I first saw him at Kelso races he wore the Northumberland livery, a blue coat with a silver crescent on his arm".

37

Apart from his fame as a piper and his notoriety as a sheepstealer and horse thief who had escaped the gallows, James is remembered as one of the first breeders of these terriers. The Allens supplied terriers to Ned Dunn of Whitlea, and James Davidson (the original character for Dandie Dinmont in the novel "Guy Mannering") of Hindlee in turn had terriers from Dunn. An endearing fact about Piper Allen is that he refused the life tenancy of a farm from the Duke of Northumberland in exchange for one of his terriers.

Stonehenge, the noted canine historian, tells in his discourse on the Dandie Dinmont Terrier in "The Dogs of The British Isles", 1872, "in these times (at the end of the last century"—i.e. around 1790) "another race of terriers, analogous to the real pepper-and-mustard was common on the Border. It is not yet extinct. It was nearly like a Dandie on long legs, but a shorter body, and in general, a less head: it was exactly of the same colour—coat, body, head and legs being exactly as in the real pepper-and-mustard. Alliances with these were not uncommon with Dandie Dinmont himself; and Tuggin or Tuggim (James Davidson's first terrier) was of this race".

He goes on to tell that "another race of terriers, in many points bearing a resemblance to the long-legged Bedlington, were often crossed with the Dandie; but even then any real judge at once knew the one breed from the other. Some of the terriers bred on Whitlea, Aiks & Co. had large long bodies, and some would be twelve inches or more sometimes in height, and would weigh from twenty to thirty pounds". These dogs certainly must have had massive bodies as a Border of twelve inches normally would not weigh more than about eighteen pounds at the maximum. However, I do know one who weighs twenty-five pounds, and although one would call him strongly built, he does not appear enormous.

Referring to Tuggin we learn that "in the year 1881 Andrew Armstrong presented a young sportsman James Davidson, with a hound and a Terrier named Tuggin, and shortly afterwards he received from a Dr. Brown of Bridgeward, the famous bitch Tar and a dog called Pepper. Tuggin was of a breed common in that wild country, a dog that could make his way anywhere, a compact, tallish Terrier, red ochre in colour with wiry hair.

"The other two were the start of the Dandies, I gather, being small, short-legged, long bodies, large long heads, and ears large and pendant, like a hound or Beagle but more pointed at the lower end."

Further light is thrown upon the terriers owned by James Davidson by a report in "British Dogs" by Hugh Dalziel, 1889, as follows: "Mr. James Scott of Newstead, speaking from a personal acquaintanceship with Davidson and his dogs, says that he had two varieties, one large and leggy, the other short on the foreleg and small and that it was only the latter that Davidson would allow to be called the Dandie Dinmont. Hugh Parry of Leaderfoot and Ned Dunn of Whitlea had a strain of these terriers from Davidson."

It is impossible to dissociate the origins of the Border Terrier from the history of the Robson and Dodd families and the Border Foxhounds. These families have been well known and respected as sportsmen and farmers for centuries. Jacob Robson's son John became Master of the Border Foxhounds in 1857. The name was given to the pack formed then by amalgamating the pack of Mr. John Robson of East Keilder with that of Mr. John Dodd of Catcleugh. The new pack was kennelled at Byrness in Redesdale and hunted by Mr. Dodd. At that time they hunted hare up to the New Year and then fox. From 1887 Mr. Jacob Robson was Master and hunted hounds; in 1919 Mr. Simon Dodd of Catcleugh joined him as Joint-Master. After having hunted hounds for forty-seven seasons, in 1926 Mr. Jacob Robson handed over the horn to his son, Mr. Jacob Robson, Jnr., who was also acting Master for his father until his father's death in 1933 after fifty-four seasons of mastership. Mr. Jacob Robson then became Joint-Master with Mr. Simon Dodd. On the death of Mr. Dodd in 1949 Mr. Robson continued as Master for another two seasons and then handed over to a Committee, himself remaining as acting Master until 1954 when Mr. Ian Hedley took over the Mastership and the horn. The Robson and Dodd families were related, John and Jacob Robson each marrying sisters of Mr. J. T. Dodd of Riccarton, and he marrying a Miss Robson. Members of the Robson family were also Masters, at some time or other, of the North Tyne and Liddesdale packs. The Robsons hunted the North Tyne country in the 1720s!

Only Borders were used with the Border Foxhounds, and they were bred to traverse this rugged country (lying on the borders of Northumberland and Roxboroughshire), after a horse, and then to bolt, or if necessary to kill and draw, the hill foxes.

Mr. Jacob Robson, Snr., wrote of his hounds in 1912: "We don't like them too heavy for the hill country, and light coloured ones are preferred. Hounds must be fast, and when they are lightly built, they last much longer; for heavy hounds do not last long on the hills, and are too slow." This maxim would apply also to the terriers who were expected to keep up with the hunt over this country. They were never carried on horseback in this district unless injured or sick.

These terriers were then found to be proficient when put to otter and badger—the former chiefly through the Northern Counties Otterhounds under the mastership of Mr. Tom Robson, and also through their connection with the Dumfries Otterhounds where they have been used for nearly sixty years. Indeed the first Border to win a Challenge Certificate was Tinker, owned by Miss Bell-Irving, and worked with the Dumfries.

As the Border was bred by farmers and shepherds to control the foxes, I suspect that they were treated as sheepdogs and would be expected to live chiefly by scavenging around the farm. Hence the reason for their ability to put on weight all too readily when fed good food. I also imagine that they would be used to fill the pot for the shepherd's family and that this accounts for their inborn game-finding sense.

Mr. Jacob Robson wrote, sometime about 1896: "These terriers have been kept in the Borders for a very long time now, but the name "Border Terrier" is of quite recent date, being given to them because they were bred and kept mostly in the English and Scottish Border districts. They have always been bred for their working qualities, and are used with the Border Foxhounds and North Tyne Foxhounds chiefly. Redewater, North Tyne, Coquet and the Scottish Borders are the districts where they are primarily bred. My father, when he lived at East Keilder, had some very high class representatives of the breed—about the years 1840–1850. Also Mr. Hedley, Bewshaugh, Mr. Sisterton, Yarrow Moor, Mr. Oliver of Spittisheugh, Mr. Elliot of Hindhope, Mr. Robson, Neeton, the Scotts and Ballantynes of Liddesdale, Mr. Dodd, Riccarton, Mr. Charlton, Chirdon, and Mr. James Patterson, Snabdough, were all noted men. At present good terriers are bred by Messrs. T. Robson, Bridgford, Anthony Dagg, Gowanburn, Thos. Hall, Lightpipe, John Hall, Larriston, Dodd, Riccarton and others.

"My father and the late Mr. Dodd, Catcleugh, preferred this breed of terrier to any other for bolting foxes, their keenness and gameness making them very suitable for the purpose. They vary in weight a good deal, although 15 to 18 lbs. is the best size, as, when bigger, they cannot follow their fox underground so well, and a little terrier that is thoroughly game is always best. Flint, a mustard dog we had here nearly thirty years ago, was small but the best bolter of foxes I ever saw. He was slow in entering to fox but when he did begin was so thoroughly game and keen that he never failed to oust his fox. The favourite colour is red or mustard, although there are plenty of the variety pepper-coloured and a few black and tan. Their coat or hair should be hard, wiry and close so as to enable them to withstand wet and cold. They should stand straight on their legs and have a short back, not made like the Dandie Dinmont, long backed and crooked. A strong jaw is a good point; not nearly so long in the nose as a Dandie or Scottish Terrier. They may be either red or black nosed, but the red nosed ones are often the keenest scented.

"I have been told that the terriers owned by Ned Dunn, Whitelea, Redewater, were more of the type of the Border than the Dandie Dinmont, and I rather think, from what my father told me, that the Dandie of fifty or more years ago resembled the Border Terrier in many respects—more so at any rate than they do now. My brother has a painting of a well known North Tyne character "Yeddie" Jackson, in his possession, painted 1820 or 1830, with a fox hound and a terrier with him, and the latter is the very type of terrier we still have. Jackson went by the name of "Hunting King" in North Tyne and Liddesdale."

Mr. Jim Dodd, joint master of the Haydon, and well known for his greyhounds and working Borders which included Ch. Dandy of Tynedale and Ch. Grakle, found a letter in a book belonging to his grandfather, from Mr. Davidson of Hyndlee in which Mr. Davidson mentioned the mating of two game red terriers—"twa real devils o'Terriers that has hard, wiry coats and would worry any damned thing that creepit."—the letter dated 1817. Mr. Dodd thought that Borders were a direct cross between the Bedlington and the Dandie Dinmont, both about 15½ lbs. in weight.

From Mr. Carruthers of Featherstone we learn "the Border Terrier owes his origin to what is known as the Whitlee breed; these terriers, my father's uncle, William Carruthers, in 1837 described as belonging to workmen at the Carter Fell lime kilns, also the Rooken Edge in Redesdale. The breed originally came from Holystone in Coquetdale, a place renowned for its terriers. The kilns have long ago been laid in and it was left to the followers of what we now know as the Border Foxhounds to carry on the breed".

Previously known as Coquetdale Terriers, they became known as Border Terriers around 1880.

A similar terrier was reported in the Livestock Journal of 1840, referred to as "a breed of hard-bitten little dogs, varying from twelve pounds to nineteen pounds in weight, and kept entirely for work. They were chiefly found in the neighbourhood of Wasdale, Drigg and Beckermet, and districts of the Lakes not usually visited by English tourists. They were fawn or red in colour, but some a black-grizzle or a dark pepper-and-salt, and some had a tinge of tan. Their coats were similar to the coat of a wire-haired terrier". This may be a reference to an early Border, or an early Lakeland, as the locality might suggest. However there are frequent references to "the Terrier of Westmoreland and Northumberland" about that time in various books and articles.

Rawdon Lee in "Modern Dogs" mentions these terriers from "Westmoreland", and also refers to the similarity between Borders and the well known strain owned by the Cockerton family (extremely well known in all sporting circles in Cumberland and Westmorland), and also those owned by the gunpowder makers at Elterwater, which were used for otterhunting, and also for despatching the greyhound foxes, marts and stoats in the district. In early references to these terriers they are described as being yellow in colour, while Mr. Jacob Robson described Flint as being mustard coloured.

It has also been suggested, indeed it caused a sensation in the breed when it was suggested in 1920, that the terriers bred at Lowther, in Cumberland, were either Borders or ancestors of the Border. A copy of the Standard was sent to Lord Lonsdale ("Lordy"—The Yellow Earl) in 1920, who wrote that there had been a strain of similar terriers at Lowther since 1732—and indeed that there was a picture at Barleythorpe depicting the Cottesmore hounds in 1693 with two of these terriers, blue in colour. Lord Lonsdale continued that the colours were white, blue, very light tan or dark brindled. This closely guarded strain were known as Ullswater Terriers.

On studying the pedigree of North Tyne Gyp, born 1917, one notes that his sire Geoff was out of a bitch Wasp, unregistered, bred by the legendary huntsman of the Ullswater Foxhounds, Joe Bowman. It is known that Lord Lonsdale followed the Ullswater Foxhounds and greatly admired Joe Bowman. The breeding of Wasp reads "Ullswater Jack ex Ullswater Nellie". Joe Bowman was known for his Patterdale Terriers which appear in the illustrations in his biography, there being made no mention of any Border Terriers as such, although there is one photograph, alas rather indistinct, which might include a Border.

Local memory, usually very reliable, refutes the suggestion that Joe Bowman ever owned a Border. He had red Lakelands, the ancestors of the present day Patterdale Terriers, which were undocked, but people who knew him and his terriers well say that he never had a Border in his kennel.

A Mr. Basley of Carlisle is reported to have had a dog in Carlisle in 1920 of the Lowther Castle strain which was a red grizzle, about $13\frac{1}{2}$ inches high, with a short strong muzzle, small dark ears, good bone, and no white on it, which appeared to be a very typical Border.

James Garrow, the colourful all-round judge of such great knowledge, reported that he saw the Ullswater Terriers at Lowther, and that they were blue or white with very dense coats. He himself was very strongly connected with the Border Terrier world and obviously he never considered that the Lowther Terriers were Borders, but he did wonder whether they were used in producing the Border. It is thought that at some stage at least one white terrier was introduced, possibly to improve the coat, and from this the white toes and shirt front still appear.

1 Thomas Heaton with his first dog, Typhoon.
Borders fulfil the important post of first dog
with tremendous success, being game for anything.

The Long Jump.

Bermudan Ch.
Hawkesburn Blue
Briar, C.D.,
demonstrating that
it is possible to
train Borders to
high standards for
obedience
qualifications.

3   This beautiful bitch, Fully Fashioned,
answers the standard in every detail and is
a fine example of the outstanding type bred by
Mr. Adam Forster—A true Border who proved
herself as a great brood bitch.

4   The head should be like that of an otter,
moderately broad in skull, with a short, strong muzzle.

5 Ch. Wharfholm Warrant with the typical, keen expression. Note the shape of the eye, the set of the ears, the well-developed nostrils and the strength in the foreface and jaw.

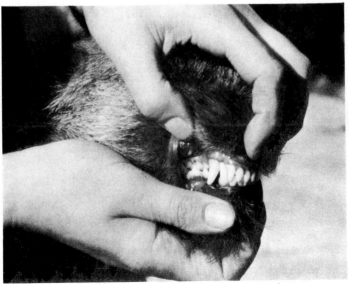

6 The correct bite and full dentition with forty-two large, strong and even teeth.

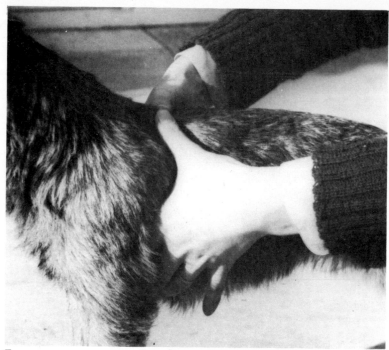

7 A terrier should be capable of being spanned by both hands behind the shoulder.

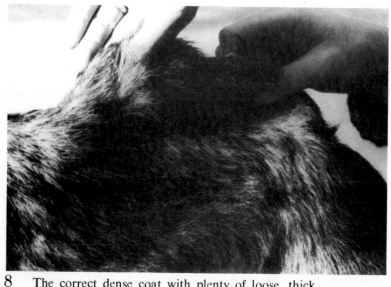

8 The correct dense coat with plenty of loose, thick skin demonstrated on Ch. Oxcroft Pearl of Mansergh.

It is known that Borders were crossed with both Lowther Terriers and Fox Terriers, and that when mated to a white terrier they threw Border coloured puppies, maybe with a little white on the chest or feet. North Tyne Gyp is reputed to have thrown puppies with white toes, and with very large, untypical feet. It was known that Ch. Ben of Tweeden descended from a Smooth Fox Terrier.

As far as can be traced, the first Border to be shown was Bacchus, at a show held in Newcastle upon Tyne in the 1870s, where he competed without success in a variety class. He was exhibited by Bill Hedley of Rothbury who was kennelman for a famous kennel of Bedlingtons. Apparently the breed was not shown again for several years.

Mr. George Davidson who judged the breed in 1920 said that he showed his first Border at an Agricultural Show in the Border country around 1880.

Captain Hamilton, owner of Ch. Blister, remembered seeing four of the breed at Kelso show in the summer of 1896. The judge was Bobbie Chapman, they were all red, and three out of the four were undershot!

Mr. F. W. Morris of Bardon Mill on Tyne saw Borders exhibited at local shows by shepherds many years later. According to him, the first show to schedule the breed was at Byrness. Mr. Tom Robson, master of the North Tyne Foxhounds, had the breed scheduled at Bellingham show in 1881. This show later became the Mecca of the Border Terrier fancy, a win here holding more prestige than one at Crufts. It was indeed a sorry day for the breed when the classes were cancelled, and, although a few classes are now scheduled, I doubt if the show will ever regain its status in the Border world. Little did the general committee know what an atrocity they perpetrated in axeing those classes.

We are told that the winner at Bellingham in the 1880s, judged by Mr. Hedley (of Bacchus fame?), was a broken coated animal of a rather nondescript type! The next report which I can find is of that show in 1907 where a Mr. Hedley again judged, with Mr. Charlton. The classes were confined to the hill districts and the dogs did not need to be registered. Twenty-four Borders were entered in the two classes. The winners are not included in the report—indeed it would be of little interest anyway as the dogs were usually listed just by the owner's name, or by the owner's name and the pet name of the dog.

The following year the classes were judged by "the Liddesdale hill men", namely W. Barton and D. Ballentyne. Again, we do not know the winners, but a famous dog man, ex-Provost Dagleish, took the opportunity of going over the Borders (which for very many years were tied to stakes in the ground at this and most other shows) and he said they had long bodies, short legs, many flesh coloured noses, light eyes predominated, coats were long and soft and light in colour. This makes one wonder why they persisted as a show proposition, and also what was introduced to improve on these dogs, or whether it was done by skilful breeding alone.

The aforementioned Mr. Morris, although a highly controversial judge by all accounts, did sterling work for the breed by keeping it in the public eye with regular articles in "Our Dogs" through the foresight of the editor, Mr. Marples, who himself owned a Border.

In 1913 the first Border Terrier was registered with the Kennel Club, a blue and tan dog, the details of which read in the Kennel Gazette: "Moss Trooper (The) d. Miss M. Rew's, by Sly (unr.)—Mr. J. Robson's Chip. Feb 2 1912". This appeared under "Any Breed or Variety of British, Colonial or Foreign Dog—Not Classified."

A total of 41 Border registrations were made in this section between 1912 and 1919 inclusive. An application for a separate breed register was submitted to the Kennel Club in 1914 and rejected. More Borders might have been registered at this time but for the widespread misunderstanding of the fact that the parents need not be registered—many people thinking that only the progeny of registered stock were eligible for registration. Once the breed gained official recognition in 1920, dogs born between 1917 and 1919, unless "bred under licence of the Kennel Club", were required to be entered for shows as Not For Competition only.

On June 24 1920 a gathering of breed enthusiasts met at Hawick to form the Border Terrier Club. It is reported that many arguments for and against the Club were aired. Mr. John Dodd of Riccarton with many supporters arguing that the breed would be ruined, and the working characteristics lost if it became a "show" dog. They finally withdrew their opposition, and agreed to cooperate with John and Jacob Robson in drawing up a Standard of points. The honorary Secretary was Mr. Hamilton Adams of London. Mr. Jasper Dodds was the first Chairman. All the Vice-Presidents were well known Masters of Foxhounds. At this meeting five Masters became members of the Club and were determined to maintain the working tradition of the breed. The Committee included Messrs. W. Barton, J. Carruthers, R. T. Elliot, J. R. Haddon, G. Sordy, John Robson, and other equally well known pillars of the breed.

In the rules were the following:—

"No show shall be supported that does not provide at least one class for Borders holding a Working Certificate." and "Every hunt in the North shall have a representative on the Committee."

History does not relate whether these rules were ever enforced, or merely proved to be highly laudable but impracticable ideals. They no longer appear in the Rule

Book of the Club, so must have died the death some-where along the way.

The Standard of points produced that day is as follows : —

"The Border Terrier is essentially a working terrier, and being of necessity able to follow a horse, must combine great activity with gameness.

N.B. The points are placed in order of their importance.

Size—Dogs should be between 14 and 17 lbs. in weight and 13 and 16 ins. in height at shoulder. Bitches should not exceed 15 lbs. in weight and 15 ins. in height at shoulder.

Head—Like that of an otter, moderately broad in skull, with short, strong muzzle, level teeth, black nose preferred, but liver or flesh coloured not to disqualify.

Eyes—Dark with keen expression.

Ears—Small V-drop.

Body—Deep, narrow and fairly long, ribs carried well back, but not oversprung, as a Terrier should be capable of being spanned by both hands behind the shoulder.

Forelegs—Straight, not too heavy in bone.

Feet—Small and catlike.

Stern—Short, undocked, thick at base, then tapering, set · high, carried gaily, but not curled over back.

Hindquarters—Racing.

Coat—Harsh and dense, with close undercoat.

Skin—Thick.

Colour—Red-wheaten, grizzle, or blue-and-tan.

Disqualification—Mouth undershot or much overshot."

When this Standard was read out at Bellingham show, Mr. J. Dodds queried the size clause, stating that the Border was a Terrier not a Whippet. The Border Terrier Club altered the weight at a later date to Dogs 13 to $15\frac{1}{2}$ lbs., bitches $11\frac{1}{2}$ to 14 lbs.

The weights of some famous Borders have been recorded. Pincher (1912) $15\frac{1}{2}$ lbs., $13\frac{1}{2}$ ins., 15 in. span; Ch. Ivo Roisterer (1915) $14\frac{1}{2}$ lbs., $12\frac{1}{2}$ ins.; Ch. Liddesdale Bess (1917) 15 lbs.; North Tyne Gyp (1917), Tinker and

Dan all 15 lbs.; Ch. Titlington Tatler (1919) 14½ lbs.; Ch. Dandy of Tynedale 15 lbs. (1921); Little Midget (1919) dam of Revenge weighed only 11 lbs. and although too small for show proved a game worker; my own Ch. Leatty Juliet of Law (1955) 14 lbs., 13½ ins.; Ch. Happy Day 15 lbs. (1959); Ch. Dandyhow Shady Knight 16 lbs. (1968).

At Bellingham, Mr. Schofield caused much merriment by referring to the "moustache" as a breed characteristic that should not be lost. Although evidently, little regard was paid to this at the time, it is gratifying to note that this point is still retained, only single-coated Borders appearing without these whiskers, although some take longer to grow them than others.

Subsequent to the forming of a Committee and drawing up an agreed Standard, a further application for a separate breed register went to the Committee of the Kennel Club on the 1st of September 1920, which was granted, as was the application to register the name "The Border Terrier Club". At this time there were some one hundred and twenty-two members of the Club. The subscription was 10/6d. for ordinary members but 2/6d. for shepherds and workmen.

Also in 1920 there was a meeting of importance in Alnwick of the Northumberland Border Terrier Club. The membership of this Club was confined to those resident in Northumberland and the Border Hunts district. The main objective appeared to further the working interests and "improve their working qualities"—was there room for improvement I wonder? I think I am correct in saying that the instigators of this Club included those who were opposed to official recognition of the breed, fearing that the working attributes would be lost. The Club kept its own stud book and a register of all terriers holding a working certificate. Unfortunately these are no longer in existence. An annual show was held where open classes were scheduled for working certificate holders, and a rule made, but I do not know how successfully, that in puppy classes the sire and dam must hold a working certificate;

49

three years' warning was given of this rule! Another rule
was "that if any part of a terrier's face was missing
through legitimate work, that part was deemed perfect".
This rule was respected, as Mr. Adam Forster's Coquetdale Vic had much of her face missing, but won at these
shows.

The President was The Duke of Northumberland,
Vice Presidents, Mr. John Robson and Masters of Fox-
hounds in Northumberland and the Border country.
Mr. Bell of Tweedmouth was the first secretary. The
Committee was to consist of two representatives from
each of the following hunts: North Northumberland,
Percy, West Percy, Morpeth, Haydon, North Tyne,
Liddesdale, Jed Forest, Buccleugh, Braes of Derwent and
Berwickshire.

The Standard agreed by the Northumberland Border
Terrier Club was as follows:—

"The Border Terrier should be a real sporting terrier, and not
too big.

1. Dogs 14 lbs. Bitches 13 lbs. maximum. (This was altered
   in 1921 to 15 lbs. and 14 lbs. respectively.)
2. Head, otter-shaped. The skull should be flat and wide.
3. The jaws powerful and not pointed.
4. Nose, black or flesh coloured.
5. Ears, small and curved rather to the side of the cheek.
6. Neck, moderate length, slightly arched and sloping grace-
   fully into the shoulder.
7. Not too long and well ribbed up (body).
8. Chest, narrow.
9. Shoulders, long, sloping, and set well back.
10. Legs, true and muscular, and not out at the elbow.
11. Coat, wiry and hard with good undercoat.
12. Tail, well carried and not over the back.
13. Mouth, level: undershot or pig jawed no use."

The first Club show held at Rothbury in April 1921
must have been a memorable occasion, judged by Mr.
John Robson, Newton, and Mr. J. T. Dodd, Riccarton.
Catalogues sold at 1/- each and prize money was first: £3,
second: £2 and third: £1—better than a present day

championship show! A huge entry of 103 dogs was made by 77 exhibitors who included Earl Percy and Lord Hugh Percy. Their father, the Duke of Northumberland, attended the show. Four dogs were entered Not for Competition, under the rule about having been registered previous to 1920. The Open Dog class had 36 entries, including the winner, Titlington Tatler, and such names as Tinker, High Newton Flint, Dan, Dash, Tweedside Red Type, Ingram Beetle, Carruther's Flint, North Tyne Gyp, Grip of Tynedale and Ivo Roisterer. The eight classes scheduled: puppy six to nine months, puppy nine to twelve months, a Standard weight class (entrants to be over twelve months) and open, for each sex. Many other famous dogs and personalities attended this show, and should I ever be granted a trip backwards through time I shall toss a coin to see whether I pop in on the Court of Queen Elizabeth I or visit this Border show at Rothbury.

Titlington Tatler, considered to be the outstanding dog of his time, and one of the best there had been to date, went unplaced at Bellingham the month after triumphing at this great show—rien ne change!

Mr. Bell resigned as secretary in 1928 and Mr. Tom Ferguson took over with Mrs. Neilson as treasurer. However, Mr. Ferguson died very suddenly and the Club appeared to die with him. Mrs. Neilson made an unsuccessful attempt to gather the remaining Committee members together. The Club records unfortunately were lost as were those earlier ones of The Border Terrier Club.

The Border Terrier Club is, of course, the "parent" Club, but three other Clubs have been formed to cover regional activities. It should be clearly understood that the Border Terrier Club is the breed Club for the United Kingdom, not for the Border counties, as many people erroniously believe.

The Southern Border Terrier Club was founded in 1930, and for many years has produced an interesting year book and also keeps a register of all holders of Working Certificates issued by the Club. In it's early days this Club was known as The Southern Counties Border Terrier Club.

The Northern Border Terrier Club was founded in 1946, to cover activities in Northumberland and Durham. This Club was granted Championship Show status in 1973.

The Yorkshire, Lancashire and Cheshire Border Terrier Club was founded in 1955 to serve those counties, but unfortunately support from Cheshire dwindled so the activities were centred more on Yorkshire and Lancashire. Championship status was granted in 1961.

These four Clubs cover most areas with their activities, and are all extremely well supported. Their functions include shows, match meetings, and social gatherings, as well as recording working certificates. Apart from scheduling working classes at their shows, and encouraging their members to work their dogs and helping whenever possible, there is little concrete that can be done to help the working enthusiasts as any form of working terrier trial is illegal in the United Kingdom. However, by continuing to encourage and support, and participate in as much as possible, the working side, these clubs endeavour to maintain the aims and ideals of the Masters of Foxhounds gathered at Hawick in 1920. May the future of the breed be as creditable as its past.

CHAPTER 5

The Influence of Bloodlines and Kennels

The previous chapter told of the great influence on the breed from the early dogs owned by the Robsons, Elliots, Dodds, Daggs and the other early breeders. These dogs appear right back in the pedigrees, and are difficult to sort out as they were unregistered, and therefore difficult to identify.

The same names recur, for instance Wasp unr. by Ullswater Jack out of Ullswater Nellie and Wasp unr. by Rock out of Fury; Ginger (1910), Ginger unregistered 1924 and Ginger unregistered.

To confuse even further, the same dog may appear with more than one name, as it was permissible to change a dog's name completely. Examples of this are North Tyne Gyp who also appeared as Gyp, Ch. Ivo Roisterer was was previously known as Mick, and Ch. Wedale Jock who was Craig Ian.

The fact that there is a strange tradition that the great Border breeders do not use a prefix also makes it very difficult to tell the strain, ownership or even locality of the dog in question. Mr. John Renton and Mr. Wattie Irving never used a prefix, neither did Mr. Adam Forster, although the dogs bred by the Forster family in later years bore the initials "F.F." in their name—for example Frugal Friar and Fully Fashioned. However, even this is not a safe conclusion to draw as others on occasion also used these initials. For many years Mrs. Sullivan did not use a prefix for her Dandyhow kennel, but they can be recognised by the initials "B.S." in their names—

53

Bette's Survivor, Beautiful Spy and Brins Selection are all wellknown examples.

Bearing these points in mind, I am now going to try to trace the influences of some of the famous dogs, lines and kennels. I suggest that any reader not interested in pedigrees and ancestry, should skip this chapter! Of course it is not possible to follow this comprehensively in one chapter, and so there will of necessity be omissions of dogs and breeders. It would fill a complete book to cover this fully.

Regarding the earlier dogs, I cannot say much for the reasons given already, so I take my starting date from the first Challenge Certificates awarded in 1920, and work backwards, and forwards, from that date, as by that time more Borders were registered, and are therefore easier to trace.

The first dogs to produce consistent show stock seem to have been Titlington Jock and North Tyne Gyp. Titlington Jock, born in 1909, bred by Mr. Allgood and owned by Mr. Sordy, sired the first Champion, Teri (who sired Ch. Ivo Rarebit), and the great Ch. Titlington Tatler (sire of Ch. Tweedside Red Type and Ch. Tweedside Tatters) and Sandiman (sire of Ch. Cribden Comet). Titlington Jock was considered to have given the breed a tremendous lift by siring such great stock.

North Tyne Gyp owned by Mr. J. T. Dodd, was born in 1917. His immediate progeny included Tinker (3 C.C.s), Ch. Dandy of Tynedale, Ch. Daphne, Ch. Themis (the dam of Ch. Tertius), and Ch. Grip of Tynedale (sire of Ch. Scarside Belle and Ch. Barney Bindle). North Tyne Gyp was descended from Joe Bowman's Ullswater Jack and Nellie, about whom there is the uncertainty of whether they were Borders or Patterdale Terriers. He was responsible for good heads but passed on his own poor front, and threw poor feet which were very often white.

Mr. W. Barton's name may not be so familiar as the names of his dogs, which appear behind many pedigrees.

He was the owner of the dogs in an early group photograph, Venom, Venus, Viper, Piper, etc. His first was Bess I, bred by Mr. J. Dodd in 1900. From her many Borders descend in unbroken line. Her own pedigree traces back on one line to Mr. Robson's Flint 1878. Mr. Barton's Borders were noted for their gameness, Bess he considered the gamest. Her daughter Venus, which Mr. Barton considered the best he ever bred, did a considerable amount of winning at agricultural shows, and was the first Border to win a Challenge Cup, in 1913. From Venus came Piper and Daisy in 1916, Piper being the sire of Liddesdale Nailer and Scamp. Liddesdale Nailer sired the first ever bitch to win a Challenge Certificate who became the first bitch Champion in the breed, Ch. Liddesdale Bess, owned by Mr. Barton, who described her thus "a grand little bitch, short coupled, dark red with a short thick set coat with hair like wire, she stood on her legs like a thoroughbred horse and had feet like a cat. She also had the flat otter skull". She took her first C.C. under Mr. S. Dodd at the first Championship Show for the breed, the Border Terrier Club held in Carlisle in 1920. She was made up at Ayr the same day as Ch. Teri became the first ever Border Terrier champion in 1921, and won her fifth C.C. when she was seven. She held a Working Certificate. A son of her's Dubh Glas, owned by Miss Rew, the first person to register a Border, won 1 C.C. and met a nasty end, falling off a cliff working. Ch. Liddesdale Bess and Ch. Teri were mated together several times, from this mating descended Ch. Heronslea.

Others to descend from this line were Ch. Station Masher, who carried two lines to Scamp and one to Liddesdale Nailer, and her grandson Whitrope Don, from whom descended Ch. Foxlair, Foomert, Ch. Oakwood Pickle, Halleaths Piper, Miss Grakle and Stung Again (the dam of Ch. Share Pusher and Finery). Also from Ch. Station Masher descended Fully Fashioned, the celebrated brood bitch.

Mr. Barton bred Foomert, the sire of Shiel Law who sired Ch. Rising Light and was grandsire to Ch. Portholme Magic. A granddaughter of Foomert, Epigram, 2 C.C.s. was also behind Ch. Rising Light.

The lines of Titlington Jock and North Tyne Gyp were combined and bred Ch. Tweedside Red Topper (Ch. Dandy of Tynedale, by Gyp, ex Ch. Tweedside Red Tatters, by Jock), Ch. Tertius, Ch. Rustic Rattler, Ch. Benton Biddy, Ch. Station Masher, Ch. Ben of Tweeden and Ch. Twempie Tinker, amongst others.

In 1916 Mr. Adam Forster bred two litter sisters. One, Gippy, was the dam of Ch. Titlington Tatler. The other, Coquetdale Vic, did a tremendous amount of winning including winning outright the cup given by the Northumberland Border Terrier Club for the best dog or bitch by winning it three times, the last time after she had been badly disfigured by work. Her first litter to Ch. Ivo Roisterer, owned at that time by Mr. Forster's father-in-law, Mr. Carruthers, consisted of Flint (winner of the C.C. on his only outing, owned by Mr. Jack Carruthers) and Col. Appleyard's Dash and Ch. Winnie. Flint sired Rab o'Redesdale who sired that important dog, Rival. Mated to Titlington Jock, Coquetdale Vic bred Little Midget, a very game little terrier, and she bred Revenge.

Both these remarkable dogs were owned by Adam Forster. Rival was bred by his brother-in-law Mr. Jack Carruthers, and was swapped for a bitch puppy, while Revenge was sold and returned to him in exchange for a bitch—on such events hang the threads of Border history!

Revenge (1922—Buittie ex Little Midget) sired Chs. Blister, Todhunter, Happy Mood, Bladnoch Raider, and Benton Biddy. Ch. Blister won 14 C.C.s and 2 reserve C.C.s at seventeen shows, lived nearly fifteen years and sired Ch. Not So Dusty and Stingo, (the sire of Ch. Share Pusher and Ch. Finchale Lass).

Rival (1924 Rab o'Redesdale—Tibby unr.) produced only one Champion, but a good one, Ch. Ranter who sired Ch. Grakle (sire of Ch. Oakwood Pickle) and Gem of Gold (sire of Ch. Dinger who sired Ch. Barb Wire and Ch. Brimball of Bridge Sollers, for many years the record holder in the Breed, winning 15 C.C.s).

A logical step was to breed these lines together and from this comes virtually every present day Border Terrier. By doing this in a simple way such dogs as Ch. Barb Wire, Ch. Gay Fine, Ch. What Fettle, Ch. Aldham Joker and Ch. Finchale Lass were produced. On tracing back the lines of famous stud dogs, one finds the Rival and Revenge lines occurring again and again. Ch. Future Fame's extended pedigree includes nine lines to Rival, four to Revenge and one to Little Midget, the dam of Revenge. This makes a total of fourteen lines to Coquetdale Vic!

Mr. J. T. Dodd, of Hexham, owned many top class Borders over a great many years. He owned the great sire, North Tyne Gyp, and Ch. Dandy of Tynedale. In partnership with Mr. W. Carruthers he owned Ch. Grip of Tynedale, Ch. Grakle and the C.C. winners Allen Piper, Huntress, Foxie, Hankhams Tinker, Leu In and Queen of the Hunt.

In 1920 Mr. G. Thompson bred Ch. Themis. From her came Ch. Tertius and the C.C. winning Kimley Lass. Tertius sired Ch. Troglodyte. This line then seemed to disappear.

The first Champion Border was Ch. Teri, born in 1916, owned and bred by Mr. T. Lawrence. A red dog by Titlington Jock, he was considered very sound but rather large, weighing 17 lbs. He sired Ch. Ivo Rarebit and the C.C. winner Ivo Rally, but his greatest influence comes through the line from his son, Riccarton Jock to Rab o'Lammermoor, from which the majority of Borders descend. His mother, Tib unregistered, was sold to Mr. Lawrence, a relief Stationmaster at Newcastleton Station, for $4\frac{1}{2}$d by a shepherd who wanted a railway ticket!

Ch. Ivo Roisterer, bred by Mr. A. Drummond, was sold to Mr. Carruthers. As "Mr. Carruthers' Mick" he was shown at a Border show in 1919 and bought for £25 by Mr. Hamilton Adams, in the hopes that he would help popularise the Breed in the South. Apart from the litter out of Coquetdale Vic which have such a lasting influence, he sired the C.C. winners Shottun Rogue, Minden Mulberry and Tug, the sire of Coquetdale Reward (the dam of Ch. Ranter). A dead game terrier, he had an excellent nose and was used for rough shooting as he would face any cover, excelling in thorns and gorse. Several of his progeny were given to M.F.Hs. who complained that they were too hard, killing their foxes instead of bolting them, and that they were chopped by excited hounds because of their colour—a common myth in the south where they were not used to red terriers at that time. When Mr. Hamilton Adams went to India in 1923 he gave his dogs to his friend Capt. Silver (prefix Minden). Poor Roisterer was killed soon afterwards by a motor cycle.

Mr. W. Watson bred and owned Ch. Scarside Bell, born 1923. He also bred the C.C. winners Whinspear and Whinscar in 1923. Ch. Bell mated to Ch. Cribden Comet bred for him Ch. Betty of Scarside. Ch. Bell and Whinspear in 1928 bred a C.C. winner Whinstone. A son of his, Whinsnade, was a C.C. winner in 1932.

The Titlington prefix is a famous one in the breed. Owned by Mrs. G. Sordy, these were game workers. There was of course, Titlington Jock, the great sire, born 1909. He sired Ch. Teri, Ch. Titlington Tatler, Sandiman, the C.C. winners Titlington Tartar and Redden, also Crosedale Judy (the dam of Ch. Rustic Rattler). Ch. Titlington Tatler was considered one of the very best Borders there had been. He held a working certificate and sired Mrs. Black's Champions Tweedside Red Tatters and Red Type. A high price of £400, (enormous for that time) was refused for him, and he died of poison shortly afterwards. Titlington Tartar sired the C.C. winning

Twempie Twink. Another famous dog from this kennel was Titlington Peter, of whom there is a tale in the working chapter in this book. So many famous dogs descend from the Titlingtons, and their line continues down to the present day Borders.

The Tweedside prefix of Mrs. David Black was well known in Bulldogs and Borders. Her first Border Champion was Ch. Tweedside Red Tatters, born 1921, followed by her full, and older, brother, Ch. Tweedside Red Type. Mrs. Black then bred Ch. Tweedside Red Topper from Tatters, and the C.C. winning Tweedside Red Sensation. Tweedside Red Tunney was by Topper, and Television was line-bred to him, both these dogs being C.C. winners. The line from Topper carried down through Tweedside Red Trumpeter, Trumps, Bessie and Cherrie to Ch. Tweedside Red Silvo, born 1947. Mrs. Black had the distinction of winning a C.C. at Crufts for four consecutive years, 1923–1926 with either Tatters or Topper. After the war, Mr. Black had the prefix. He purchased Ch. Aldham Joker from Mrs. Twist, and by Joker out of Felton Gem bred Tweedside Red Playboy (sire of Ch. Gay Hussar, Ch. Highgarphar Sensation and Ch. Tweedside Red Gloria) and Tweedside Red Silver who sired Ch. Tweedside Red Silvo. Another by Ch. Aldham Joker, Ch. Tweedside Red Biddy, mated to Ch. Silvo, bred the C.C. winner Tweedside Red Paljoy. Ch. Silvo also sired Ch. First Choice and Ch. Tweedside Red Glamorous, the dam of Ch. Tweedside Red Dandy, the C.C. winner Tweedside Red Rusty and the famous sire Tweedside Red Kingpin — these three all being by Ch. Girvanside Cruggleton Don. Mr. McConnell, Girvanside worked closely with Mr. Black and they exchanged bitches from time to time. Kingpin sired Ch. Rab Roy, Ch. Brieryhill Gertrude, Ch. Bright Light, Ch. Barnikin and Ch. Happy Day. Other breeders to use the Tweedside blood to advantage have been Miss Bolton with Ch. Leatty Emblewest Betsy, Emblewest Ghana and Yana, and Mrs. Evelyn Hutchinson with Ch. Bolt On, bred by Miss Bolton, and Ch. Gay Lord, and Mrs. Simpson with her Solway kennel. The Tweedside blood appears in most pedigrees somewhere, and traces straight back to the first of the prefix.

Mr. J. Smart owned the Twempie prefix, and his first Champion was Twempie Tinker born in 1927, by Twempie Twink. The influence of Coquetdale Vic and her litter brother, Tino, played a strong hand in the success of this line. From Twempie Nell, Mr. Smart bred Ch. Twempie Tishy. Mr. Smart had the honour of winning both the C.C.s at Crufts in 1931, under Mr. Calvert Butler. Miss Fair (Ravensdowne prefix) took the dogs to the show for Mr. Smart, went to have a quick cup of tea before judging, and came back to find it all over, her two charges both having the C.C. over their bench, one of Messrs. Spratts attendants having handled them to their success! Tishy mated to Ch. Blister bred Twempie Tony, sire of Verdict who was sire of Ch. Rising Light and grandsire of Ch. Portholme Magic.

The influence of the Forster family and their Borders is outstanding, and without them the present Border might have been very ordinary. Their influence stretches from Coquetdale Vic, born 1916, to Swift and Sure, the last C.C. winner they bred in 1957—a great era. Already mentioned are Coquetdale Vic, Flint, Ch. Winnie, Ch. Ranter, Coquetdale Reward, Rival and Revenge. Others shown or bred by the family included Ch. Future Fame, Ch. First Footer, Ch. Fine Features, Ch. Hugill Sweep, Int. Ch. Lucky Purchase and the C.C. winners Miss Tut, Furious Fighter, Finery, Fire Fighter, Harbottle, Pride of Bothal and Swift and Sure. It is impossible to separate the influence of this line, as it is throughout the breed. Ch. Ranter sired Ch. Grakle (sire of Ch. Oakwood Pickle) Renton (whose son Randale sired Ch. Bess of The Hall and Ch. Teddy Boy for Miss Long) and Furious Fighter who was badly injured working and had to be withdrawn from the show ring as a result of this, after winning one C.C. He belonged to Sir John Renwick, and sired Ch. Macmerry and Osmond Fury (sire of Ch. Osmond

Braw Lad) but probably his most important progeny was Fearsome Fellow. From him came Ch. Hepple and a long line of Champions from Hepple (Ch. Cravendale Chanter, Ch. Falcliff Topper, Ch. Cravendale Copper, Ch. Falcliff Tantaliser, Ch. Yak Bob, Ch. Ribbleside Falcliff Trident, Ch. Deerstone Falcliff Ramona, Ch. Duttonlea Mr. Softy, Ch. Duttonlea Lillian, Ch. Ribbleside Ridgeman) and also Ch. Dryburn Devilina. Ch. Cravendale Copper spent his last years at Dandyhow, and his influence is beginning to show there tying in well with their bloodlines. Another by Fearsome Fellow was Ch. Deerstone Driver, sire of Ch. Wharfholm Winnie, and yet another Fire Fighter from whom descends Ch. Leatty Druridge Dazzler, sire of Ch. Leatty Lucky, Ch. Dryburn Dazzler and Ch. Leatty Loyallass.

Fully Fashioned (Fearsome Fellow ex Flamingo) proved to be a key brood bitch in the breed. To Ch. Boxer Boy she bred Fire Master, the sire of Ch. Golden Imperialist, later exported to Holland. To Ch. Future Fame, her half brother, both being by Fearsome Fellow, she bred "the Goods" as the saying goes: Ch. Lucky Purchase, exported to America; Ch. First Footer, the dam of Harbottle, two C.C.s (maternal grandsire of Chs. Brookend Baggins and Brandybuck), Ch. Eardiston Fettle (from her descend Ch. Ribbleside Ridgeman and Ch. Step Ahead), Eignwye Sally (dam of Ch. Eignwye Enchantress); and another great brood bitch, Final Flutter.

Final Flutter was the dam of Ch. Hugill Sweep, Fighting Fettle (sire of Dandyhow Brussel Sprout, Ch. Dandyhow Bitter Shandy and Dandyhow Blue Shadow), Swift and Sure, and Joyous Bet (dam of Ch. New Halfpenny). From Fully Fashioned come really lovely heads.

Another great influence from Fearsome Fellow comes through Ch. Future Fame, an outstanding sire. He sired Ch. First Footer (dam of Ch. Eardiston Fettle to whom both Ch. Ribbleside Ridgeman and Ch. Step Ahead are line bred); Int. Ch. Lucky Purchase; Ch. Fine Features; Ch. Winstonhall Knavesmire Canny Lad; Ch. Alvertune

Martin; Ch. Rayndale Ramona; Jessabelle (dam of Ch. Joytime who sired Ch. Sally Laurus, Ch. Kathyanga, and Ch. Leatty Felldyke Gorse); Maxton Red Honey (dam of Ch. Maxton Mannequin from whom came Ch. Maxton Miss Mink); Carry On (sire of Ch. Tuppence Coloured and Ch. Eignwye Enchantress); Final Flutter from whom came Ch. Hugill Sweep; and Ch. Maxton Matchless (sire of Ch. Marrburn Morag and Millbank Tarka—from Morag come Ch. Starrburn Merrymaid, Ch. Maxton Monarch and Ch. Starrburn Sultan—and from Tarka, Ch. Maxton Makrino, Ch. Maxton Marla and Oxcroft Rocket the sire of Ch. Oxcroft Vixen and Ch. Oxcroft Moonmagic). Mrs. Sullivan mated Dandyhow Brown Sherry to him and produced Dandyhow Seamus, of which more later, suffice to say here that many Champions came from this mating.

The line from Ch. Future Fame and Fully Fashioned is very strong and many of today's big winners are bred back on these lines.

Mr. Forster worked his dogs for many years, and many of the gamest terriers about nowadays are from these bloodlines. He did not like them too big, and paid particular attention to the beautiful otter heads which came from his stock.

Mr. Wattie Irving appeared on the scene some time later than Mr. Forster, in 1926 with Arnton Billy (breeder Andrew Irving) and Ch. Station Masher. Masher bred Ch. Kineton Koffee which Mr. Irving owned in partnership with Capt. C. R. Pawson, and Ch. Joyden, who won ten C.C.s, including at least one every year from 1932 until 1939 inclusive, the last being at Crufts when she was nine years old—a great record. The descent from Ch. Station Masher carries on from Stung Again and Finery to such key names as Ch. Eignwye Enchantress, Ch. Eardiston Fettle, Harbottle and Swift and Sure. Another line from Stung Again takes us to Ch. Leatty Druridge Dazzler and his many descendants. Others Mr. Irving bred or owned included Ch. Heronslea, Ch. Rising Light (ten C.Cs), Rab O'Lammermuir (sire of Ch. Fox

Lair), Ch. Alexander, Ch. Rab Roy, Ch. Brieryhill Gertrude, Ch. Bright Light (11 C.C.s), and the C.C. winners Din Shiela, Hunty Gowk (Mr. Renton's first big winner), Lady Pat, Dykebrae Devonfury, and My Beau. Surely one of the unluckiest dogs he owned was a great headed dog, Alton Lad, who won seven Reserve C.C.s, including one on the occasion when he won the Open dog class, and was then beaten by the one who was second to him, for the C.C.! Ch. Bright Light won her last C.C. in 1964, completing some 38 years of top dogs for him. Wattie Irving's dogs had no fancy presentation, being presented more or less in the rough, but they were good Borders and worth further examination.

For many years dictator in the Breed, he is sadly missed. A great character, and afraid of no man or woman, he did much for the Breed by keeping politics to the background, and the dogs to the front.

Not only could be produce good Borders, he could also produce good breeders of Borders. His son-in-law Mr. T. M. Gaddes, owning Ch. Hornpiece Salvia and breeding Ch. Hawkesburn Beaver, Wattie Irving's granddaughter, Miss Grace Gaddes, owning and making up Ch. Koffee Lad, and his grandson Mr. W. Ronald Irving, making up Ch. Bounty Tanner, owning and breeding Ch. Arnton Fell, and making up Ch. Llanishen Penelope and her daughter Ch. May Isle Misty. Like his grandfather, Ronnie Irving was honorary secretary to the Border Terrier Club for some years. He is also one of the up-and-coming all round judges. I am one of the small handful of people to have shown under three generations of Irvings, Wattie, his son Andrew, and his son Ronnie. Who knows, I may live long enough to show under four generations!

The Bladnoch prefix is another which still features very strongly behind most present day bloodlines. Dr. Lillico of Cumberland owned this prefix. The first in my records was Bladnoch Gyp, born in 1928, who mated to Ch. Ben of Tweeden, bred Bladnoch Twink, the sire of

Red Gold. Red Gold mated to Revenge produced Ch. Bladnoch Raider in 1932. A litter sister to Red Gold, Tarquair Gypsy, bred Ch. Fox Lair. Ch. Bladnoch Raider sired Ch. Gay Fine and Ch. What Fettle, and the C.C. winners Puffin and Dipley Deans. Another sister of Red Gold, owned by Mr. McEwan, who bred Red Gold, was Glentrool Dinkum, dam of Duskie Maiden, winner of two C.C.s By mating together Dipley Dusty (Glentrool Dinkum's grandson) to Bladnoch Jinty (a Fox Lair daughter and Raider granddaughter), Dr. Lillico bred Ch. Bladnoch Spaewife in 1945. She was the first Champion after the war, but died in 1947, a sad loss. In 1935 came Brownie o'Bladnoch, and he, mated to a Raider daughter, bred Bladnoch Patty. This bitch to Fox Lair bred Bladnoch Jinty (dam of Spaewife) and also Portholme Merrylegs, who bred Portholme Mab. Patty to Callum, a Fox Lair son, bred Deerstone Mischief, dam of Deerstone Defender (the first Deerstone to win a C.C. and grandsire of Ch. Portholme Manly Boy). Both Ch. Alverton Fury and Ch. Cherisette (whose dam was from a brother and sister mating) were granddaughters of Brownie: Raider was the sire of the brother and sister behind Cherisette. Other Raider granddaughters were Ch. Dronfield Berry and Ch. Girvanside Tigress Mischief. Bladnoch Brock of Deerstone (full brother to Ch. Spaewife) sired Ch. Leatty Lace. Ch. Lucy Gray, owned by Mr. McEwan, was from a bitch bred by Dr. Lilico, by Callum. Portholme Rob was also bred here—he was the sire of Nettle Tip (sire of Ch. Portholme Maire and Ch. Portholme Mamie) and grandsire of Ch. Portholme Marthe of Deerstone. Ch. Deerstone Driver was out of Bladnoch Tinker Bell, litter sister to Brock. Ch. Fine Features, Ch. Girvanside Cruggleton Don and Ch. Chalkcroft Fancy also bore Bladnoch blood, as do so many of today's dogs, chiefly through the Deerstone, Portholme and Wharfholm stock, and also the many descendants of Tweedside Red Kingpin (sired by Ch. Girvanside Cruggleton Don). Dr. Lilico was indeed a clever breeder, as will be realized if the pedigree of his dogs are studied carefully.

Mr. Johnson held a very strong hand in Borders in the early 1930s. He bred a very lovely bitch, Ch. Not So Dusty, a wheaten, in 1932, out of Hunty Gowk (bred by Wattie Irving), by Ch. Blister (by Revenge). This bitch won eight C.C.s, but was unfortunately a non-breeder. She met a sad end as she was lost when quite old and never heard of again. Using a Rival son on Hunty Gowk, he bred Red Floss, a very ugly bitch which he considered spoilt the look of the kennel. She was given away to a miner, in whelp, on condition that Mr. Johnson should have the litter, by Ch. Bladnoch Raider—there were only two puppies, Ch. Gay Fine and Ch. What Fettle. In his latter years. Ch. What Fettle lived with Miss Garnett Orme, who kept him through the war. Ch. Bladnoch Raider joined Mr. Johnson's kennel. Mr. Thompson Coates handled some of these dogs to their wins, as he was then employed by Hildebrand Wilson, a professional handler. In these days the dogs were often sent by rail to the show and handled by anyone available upon arrival—those in the care of a professional handler were very lucky dogs.

Mr. John T. Renton, the third of the legendary figures of Messrs. Adam Forster, Wattie Irving and John Renton, arrived on the scene slightly later than Wattie Irving. In fact the first bitch with which he won a C.C. was Hunty Gowk, bred by Wattie Irving, and sold to Mr. Johnson. He won with her in 1931, the same year that he started winning C.C.s with Ch. Todhunter, who won six C.C.s in all. The following year Ch. Happy Mood won five C.C.s, she eventually totalled 12 in all. Ch. Dinger followed in 1933. Another good dog was Dandy Marvel who won one C.C. and had to be withdrawn as he was so badly marked-up working. Others owned or bred here included Ch. Barb Wire, Ch. Rona Rye, Ch. Ranting Fury, Ch. Vic Merry, Ch. First Choice, Ch. Scotch Mist, Ch. Ranting Roving, Ch. Barnikin, Ch. Happy Day, Ch.

Handy Andy and Ch. Hawkesburn Happy Returns, also Epigram, Regal Rusty and Border Queen, all C.C. winners. Happy Returns was born in 1966, so Mr. Renton had a span of some 35 years at the top. Like the other two great pillars, Wattie Irving and Adam Forster, it is difficult to isolate the influence of his breeding, so widespread is it. Ch. Happy Day was a dog that Mr. Renton thought a great one, and he took great pleasure in the fact that this dog (weight 15 lbs.) won Best of Breed at Bellingham show for three consecutive years. Mr. Renton's dogs will always be remembered by me for their ultra-Border type and refined otter-like heads, and a particular quality about their bone which is difficult to define. It was clean, straight, strong yet not too heavy, and his dogs always had it.

Probably in recent years a breeder who had been longest in the Breed was Miss Helen Vaux. Her first Champion, Dryburn Kutchuk, whelped 1927, won his and Miss Vaux's first C.C. in 1929. Her next Champion was Ch. Oakwood Pickle in 1934. The C.C. winning Newminster Rab then followed. From Mr. Renton she purchased Ch. Vic Merry and won further honours with her. In 1952 she made up Ch. Dryburn Devilina and the following year bred two blue and tans from her, Ch. Dryburn Dazzler and the C.C. winner Leatty Linty. The next C.C. winner was Dryburn Delphinium. Miss Vaux then stopped showing regularly, but continued to breed good stock as was proved when Mrs. Sneddon made up Ch. Newsholme Modesty, bred by Miss Vaux in 1967, and Mrs. Bulmer made up the blue and tan, Ch. Easingwold Rascal, bred by Miss Vaux, and made up in 1974—thus completing some 45 years for Miss Vaux at the top of the Border tree. She was also well known as a breeder of ponies, and at one time was in partnership with Mrs. Whitwell, I think over the Whippets if my memory serves me correctly.

Sir John Renwick, Bart. came of a great sporting family. His father was Sir George Renwick, Bart., a ship owner and M.P. for Newcastle upon Tyne. Sir John was well known as a gentleman jockey and racehorse trainer at Malton. He hunted his father's harriers as a young man and was later Master of the Staintondale and Goathland Foxhounds. He died in 1946 aged 69. His prefix, Newminster, was amongst the best respected in working terriers, work being his prime consideration, showing coming a long way behind. His first Champion was Ch. Jedworth Bunty, born 1928, who was made up in 1930. The following year Tarset Lad won two C.C.s. He bought Ch. Grakle already made up by Messrs. Dodd and Carruthers, but went on to bring his total to nine C.C.s From Adam Forster he bought a good dog, Furious Fighter. Unfortunately this dog was badly injured working, and had a wound on his face which never healed. He won one C.C. however. From a son of Ch. Jedworth Bunty, came Ch. Newminster Rose. Furious Fighter sired the C.C. winning Newminster Rab, Ch. Ranting Fury and Fearsome Fellow (the sire of the great sire Ch. Future Fame). Miss Vaux introduced a lot of Newminster blood, the two strains seem to go very well together to produce a very hard bitten, workmanlike terrier.

A cousin of Sir John was Lewis Renwick, again a keen working Border man. He owned the C.C. winning Wisp of Frimley, born 1921, and for many years worked hard for the breed.

On the death of Sir John, the title and the prefix went to his son, Sir Eustace, again a great sportsman who met his end through a hunting accident. He continued to breed and work Borders of the same line. On his death the prefix went to his daughter, Mrs. Percy, and she is continuing to breed the same strain which can be traced back over fifty years.

Other members of this family were the Rev. Renwick, Mrs. A. Williams a well known Pekingese breeder, and of course Mrs. Dorothy Whitwell, of the famous Seagift prefix, known for her lovely gundogs, Whippets and Greyhounds and a judge of the highest calibre. This family were reared on hounds, terriers, dogs and horses and fully understand the function and build of a working animal—would there were more people of this sort being bred nowadays.

The breed in the South owes a great deal to the Pawson brothers, Capt. C. R. (Kineton) and J. J. (Dipley). Bred from a Northumberland family, they knew the value of the Border as a working dog, and both bred many good dogs game and true. Ch. Kineton Koffey, owned in partnership with Mr. Wattie Irving was one of the best dogs in the South at that time (1930s). Amongst his other well known dogs were the C.C. winning Kineton Niki and Merriment. Mr. John Pawson had the distinction of owning a Waterloo Cup winner. He also owned some good Borders, breeding Callum and Ch. Dipley Dibs in 1938, and owning Ch. Copper of Dipley, Ch. Dipley Dinghy and the C.C. winners Dipley Dave, Doris and Deans. These gentlemen were chiefly responsible for founding the Southern Border Terrier Club. Many kennels built their foundations upon the Kineton and Dipley lines, including the Swallowfields owned by Lady Russell. However, the influence of these lines is pretty widespread through the influence of Callum and also through the blending of the Bladnoch and Dipley lines which are behind the Deerstone and Wharfholm strains.

Another enthusiast to bring good Bloodlines to the South has been Miss May Long. Her first Border, Randale, was bought from the north. His first Championship show proved to be a disaster as Miss Long travelled with him by train. Out of the train window he spotted a rabbit and became throughly over-excited, leaping from seat to seat, and arrived exhausted at the show (so was Miss Long after having travelled with him) where he refused to show at all and sat firmly down in the ring. However, his obvious merit was spotted and Miss Long received five offers for him that day, including one from the judge who she had thought totally unimpressed by her unco-operative dog. Both his sire and his dam were by Mr. Forster's Ch. Ranter. Miss Long bred her first Champion in 1933, Bess of The Hall, by Randale, who also sired her next Champion, Teddy Boy, also bred by her in 1933. Others he sired were the C.C. winner Winstonhall Spink, and Mrs. Mulcaster's first C.C. winner, Portholme Jan. Ch. Bess of The Hall mated to Ch. Teddy Boy bred Winstonhall Bebe with which Mrs. Twist won a C.C.. Miss Long's next Champion was Ch. Winstonhall Knavesmire Canny Lad, and then Ch. Winstonhall Counden Tim, and the C.C. winners Winstonhall Wiseman, Winstonhall Randale and Winstonhall Dipper. Dipper, born 1961, traces straight back to Randale and Bess of The Hall—seven generations in some twenty-eight years. Wiseman sired Ch. Carahall Coffee, grandsire of Ch. Hawkesburn Beaver.

From Titlington Jock (1909) in direct tail male through Ch. Teri, Riccarton Jock, Burnfoot Jock, Red Rock, Whitrope Don and Knowe Roy we come to a key dog, Rab o'Lammermoor, owned by Wattie Irving. He sired two noteworthy dogs, Ch. Fox Lair and Devonside Diversion.

Ch. Fox Lair sired Ch. Dipley Dibs (from whom descended Ch. Bladnoch Spaewife, Ch. Chalkcroft Fancy, Ch. Chalkcroft The Card, and Ch. Leatty Lace) and Callum. Callum sired a great many good dogs, amongst them Ch. Dronfield Berry, Ch. Swallowfield Nutmeg, Ch. Swallowfield Coramine, Ch. Billy Boy, Ch. Lucy Gray, Deerstone Dauntless, Ch. Girvanside Cruggleton Don and Swallowfield Salvo (sire of Ch. Hornpiece Salvia). Dauntless sired Ch. Portholme Manly Boy and the influence of Callum today comes chiefly through the descendants of Ch. Manly Boy, Ch. Billy Boy and Ch. Don.

Devonside Diversion sired one Champion, Fancy Girl of Chalkcroft, but from him through his son, Deerstone Defender, and Defender's son, Ribbleside Rodger, came Mrs. Mulcaster's two Champions, Portholme Maire and Mamie. From another son, Ribbleside Red Racquet, and his son Ribbleside Rocket, came Ch. True Temper and her daughter Ch. Full Toss, also Mrs. Holmes' litter brother and sister Champions Wharfholm Wizard and Wench. From Wizard came Ch. Wharfholm Wink, Ch. Leatty Juliet of Law and Ch. Mansergh Wharfholm Wistful, the dam of Ch. Wharfholm Wizardry and grand-dam of Ch. Wharfholm Warrant. Warrant has sired to date Ch. Wharfholm Wonderlad, Ch. Mansergh Barn Owl, Ch. Final Honour and Ch. Summer Belle, and Ch. Final Honour has sired Ch. Step Ahead—so the ring is full of descendants of the two branches of the Rab o'Lammermoor family.

Mrs. Twist, Hallbourne, has owned some of the most famous dogs in the breed, and at one time must have had one of the very strongest kennels in the country. She owned three of the most famous stud dogs in the years leading up to the war, namely Ch. Fox Lair, 1934, Ch. Wedale Jock, 1934 and Ch. Aldham Joker, 1937. Ch. Fox Lair was bought as a Champion, and his influence is already mentioned. He shares a record in the breed, by winning the C.C. at Crufts for three years in succession. Ch. Wedale Jock may not immediately appear as a sensational sire, but must have had a steady good influence as he appears behind Ch. Future Fame and Ch. Billy Boy, through his grandson, Ch. Boxer Boy. Ch. Aldham Joker was the first of the breed to win a Junior Warrant. Mrs. Twist made both him and Wedale Jock up. Ch. Wedale Jock spent the war years with Miss Duthie (Todearth), and Ch. Aldham Joker was sold after the war to Mr. David Black. He sired many Champions, and put many breeders on the right track with good stock when they were picking up the threads of breeding again after the war. Amongst his children were Ch. Hallbourne Badger (a well known worker), Ch. Hallbourne Bracket, Ch. Tweedside Red Glamourous, Ch. Tweedside Red Biddy, Ch. Boxer Boy, Ch. Copper of Dipley, Ch. Swallowfield Garry and Ch. Portholme Marthe of Deerstone. It is impossible to list all his descendants as they are legion. Ch. Hallbourne Badger Sired Ch. Hallbourne

Blue Val and Ch. Hallbourne Brick. Blue Val sired Ch. Hallbourne Constancy and Brookend Vali, the sire of Ch. Brookend Baggins and Ch. Brookend Brandybuck, who in turn sired Ch. Makerston Fox Lair. Another by Blue Val was Wharfholm Hallbourne Blue Bracelet, dam of Ch. Mansergh Wharfholm Wistful, who, mated to Ch. Brookend Baggins, bred Ch. Wharfholm Wizardry. Other dogs from this kennel included the C.C. winners Hallbourne Brandy Ball, Crofter, Blue Vinney and Builder. A strong line of blue and tan comes down from Hallbourne Blue Cinders. Mrs. Twist was an active breeder for well over thirty years.

Miss Audrey Williams' Harranby prefix also bridges the pre- and post-war period. She bred her first C.C. winner, Puffin, in 1936 by Ch. Badnoch Raider out of the C.C. winning Winstonhall Spink. The next was Harranby Brenda. In 1959 Ch. Harranby Wanda was bred and campaigned by Miss Williams. Mated to Ch. Deerstone Realization, Wanda bred an extrovert and charming dog, Harranby Quest, who sired Ch. Wharfholm Warrant, the sire of four Champions to date, and grand-sire of the great ambassador in the Terrier Groups, Ch. Step Ahead. The dam of Wanda, Harranby Pippin, mated to Ch. Wharfholm Wizard bred Wharfholm Harranby Topper, a C.C. winner and sire of Ch. Mr. Tims and the dog in Sweden who has sired so many good ones, Sw. Ch. Wharfholm Warrantop. Harranby Dai, the sire of Ch. Knavesmire Kopper, is full brother to Ch. Harranby Wanda, so this breeding appears on both sides of Ch. Step Ahead.

The first Border Terrier owned by Mrs. Phyllis Mulcaster, April Shower, was a wedding present to her. This mated to Randale, bred the first of the many Portholmes to win C.C.s, Portholme Jan, born 1934. Dr. Lilico bred Portholme Merrylegs and Portholme Rob. From Merrylegs, Mrs. Mulcaster bred Portholme Mab, a C.C. winner who went to Sweden. Her first Champion was a most lovely bitch, Ch. Portholme Magic. In my humble opinion, this is the best Border I have yet seen. Mr. Stanley Mulcaster also shared this view. Her wonderful action and soundness is something I shall never forget, nor her quality, and she was an old lady when I was lucky enough to see her. She was by Portholme Michael, out of a Rob daughter, Polly Peachum. Another bred by Mrs. Mulcaster was Sandy of Dhibban, sire of Ch. Cherisette, and his sister, Dronfield Ringlet, dam of Ch. Dronfield Berry. The original bitch-line from April Shower bred on down to Ch. Fancy Girl of Chalkcroft. In 1948 Ch. Portholme Manly Boy was born, he won five C.C.s and proved a tremendous stud force, not surprising as he descends in tail male from Ch. Fox Lair, Callum and Deerstone Dauntless. He sired Ch. Carahall Cornet, Ch. Portholme Merryman, Ch. Portholme Mirth, Ch. Deerstone Destiny, and Fighting Fettle, who sired the famous stud dog, Dandyhow Brussel Sprout. The influence of these dogs will be listed later under their prefixes. The next two Champions were the litter sisters, Ch. Portholme Maire, seven C.C.s and Ch. Portholme Mamie, granddaughters of Portholme Rob. Another of his granddaughters was Ch. Portholme Marthe of Deerstone, owned by Mr. Hall and who became Mrs. Holmes' foundation bitch. She won six C.C.s. The next was Ch. Portholme Merryman, and he sired Ch. Portholme Matinee and Ch. Portholme My Dusky Lady both owned by Mrs. Fairley. Matinee bred Ch. Portholme My Fair Lady (by Manly Boy) and My Fair Lady bred Ch. Portholme Mr. Moses also owned by Mrs. Fairley, by Portholme Mustard, an outcross dog. Mr. Moses sired Ch. Deerstone Dugmore. Ch. Portholme Mirth mated to Portholme Mask and Brush (Merryman ex a Manly Boy —Maire bitch) bred Ch. Portholme Macsleap. He sired Ch. Deerstone Douglas and Ch. Hulne Lass before joining the Dalquest kennel in U.S.A. Another Mirth daughter, Moonshine (by Mustard), bred a lovely bitch My Stella, by Merryman, who would certainly have been a Champion but died very soon after winning her second C.C.

The last to be made up by Mrs. Mulcaster was Ch. Portholme March Belle, another outcross bitch, in 1964. Other C.C. winners Mrs. Mulcaster owned or bred included Dusty Dan, Portholme Mab, Portholme Jan, Portholme Mayduke, Portholme Meroe, Portholme Mary Jane and Portholme My Della. She exported many excellent Borders to America, where the influence is as strong as it is here. Another lady who gave thirty years to the breeding of excellent stock which were renowned for their harsh coats, thick skins, good legs and feet and good movement.

Lady Russell founded her Swallowfield strain on Dipley and Kineton lines. The foundation bitch, Swallowfield Tandy, was bred by Capt. C. R. Pawson in 1935. Mated to Quest (Ch. Bladnoch Raider—Dipley Dinah), she bred Keepsake in 1937. Callum, bred by Mr. J. J. Pawson in 1938 (Ch. Fox Lair—Dipley Dinah) was purchased, as was Finchale Lass. Ch. Finchale Lass won six C.C.s in 1939, shown by Lady Russell. The war curtailed the showing activities, which deprived Callum of his title no doubt, however Ch. Finchale Lass was mated to him, and produced Swallowfield Solo. Tandy was mated to Ch. Fox Lair and from this mating descended Ch. Chalkcroft The Card and Ch. Chalkcroft Fancy. In 1944 Solo was mated to Ch. Aldham Joker and bred Ch. Swallowfield Garry, who sired Ch. Swallowfield Shindy, Ch. Swallowfield Fergus (out of a Solo granddaughter) and Swallowfield Whisper. The latter, owned by Dr. and Mrs. Cuddigan, won a C.C. and bred Ch. True Temper, who bred Ch. Full Toss, a good bitch who was unfortunately a non-breeder. Callum came through the war to sire many good dogs and progenitors of future Borders, amongst them Ch. Swallowfield Coramine, Ch. Dronfield Berry, Ch. Lucy Gray, Ch. Girvanside Cruggleton Don and the great sire, Ch. Billy Boy. Keepsake was mated to Callum and produced Swallowfield Sadie whose daughter, Hornbeam Heatherbell, put back to Callum, bred Ch. Swallowfield Nutmeg. After a long break from the show ring of some twenty years, Lady Russell made a come-back with Ch. Dandyhow Sandpiper which she purchased from Mrs. Sullivan with two C.C.s to his credit. She brought his total up to four C.C.s. He sired Mrs. Marchant's Ch. Hawkesburn Spindle. Lady Russell bought this dog because he closely resembled her past Borders, and also because he traced back to Ch. Swallowfield Garry in six generations— remarkable as Garry was born in 1944 and Ch. Sandpiper in 1968.

Miss Hester Garnett Orme was also showing pre-war. Her Raisgill prefix appears in many pedigrees the world over. Her foundation bitch, Wild Lucy, was bred by Mr. Johnson, by Ch. Bladnoch Raider ex Hunty Gowk. She bred Raisgill Rasta by Ch. Aldham Joker, and Raisgill Ribbon by Callum. From Raisgill Rasta, mated to Ch. Swallowfield Garry, she bred Ch. Swallowfield Shindy and Raisgill Roidan. Ribbon to Portholme Rob bred Nettle Tip, the maternal granddam to Chs. Portholme Maire and Mamie. Raisgill Reefer, (Ch. Aldham Joker ex Ribbon), won two C.C.s Ribbon and Ch. Chalkcroft The Card bred the C.C. winning Raisgill Romance. Ribbon and Ravensdowne Joker bred Raisgill Radella of Deerstone, from which Mr. Hall bred Ch. Deerstone Destiny and Ch. Deerstone Desirable, these two being by a descendant of Rasta, Ch. Portholme Manly Boy. Ch. What Fettle joined the Raisgills, by Ch. Bladnoch Raider ex a daughter of Hunty Gowk, and Rasta was mated to him to produce Rosa, and she with Ch. Aldham Joker bred Deerstone Ornesta, the dam of Manly Boy's sire. Mr. Williams bred his first C.C. winner out of Raisgill Rainbow, a granddaughter of Roidan. Miss Garnett Orme became more keen on the working side than the show ring, and in latter years concentrated on this, many of her dogs working with hunts up and down the country. She also worked very hard with Mrs. Twist in sorting out the early pedigrees, and became a mine of information on bloodlines, and breed records. Luckily

THE INFLUENCE OF BLOODLINES AND KENNELS

her papers and books on these are safely held by the Southern Club. She produced that excellent record of Champion and C.C. Winners Pedigrees, and was also responsible for the publication of that excellent book, Border Tales. A charming lady, with a wonderful dry wit, and a great knowledge of all there was to know about the breed, she is sadly missed and many a time I have thought "if only I could ask Hester". However the Raisgill blood lives on, and we still have available the fruits of her hard labours in recording the early Borders for which we are eternally grateful.

Another lady who has been showing Borders for some thirty-six years is Miss Nancy Turrall, Counden. Her greatest successes came after the war, following the purchase of Ravensdowne Roxana from Mrs. Twist. This bitch, mated to Ch. Billy Boy bred Ch. Counden Trudy and Ch. Winstonhall Counden Tim. These two won both C.Cs at Leeds show in 1962. Roxana mated to Ch. Hallbourne Brick bred Counden Jet, the mother of that famous worker, Hanleycastle Russ, who sired Ch. Hanleycastle Judy and Hanleycastle Jasper, (who sired Ch. Clipstone Hanleycastle Bramble). Russ is behind many working Borders. Ch. Trudy to Ch. Portholme Macsleap bred Ch. Counden Troena.

Miss Turrall is a keen hunting lady, and always has a very high class Border with her, her latest being Ch. Llanishen Rosemary of Counden, bred by Mr. Wiseman yet identical in type to Chs. Trudy and Troena.

Mr. W. Hancock was another keen working enthusiast and he, Mr. N. Fielden and Mr. M. M. Horn must have spent years of their lives down fox-holes, if the hours were totted up! He bred Mr. Fielden's great winner and worker, Ch. Vanda Daredevil in 1944, and in 1948 made up his own bitch, Ch. Alverton Fury. In 1955 he made up a dog, Ch. Alvertune Martin. He also owned the C.C. winner Alvertune Fantasy, and bred Furious Fury, the C.C. winning son of Ch. Vanda Daredevil. Mr. Horn owned and bred Ch. Hepple, a dog born in 1948 whose bloodlines were chiefly those of Messrs. W. Carruthers and Adam Forster. This dog sired Ch. Cravendale Chanter and Ch. Dryburn Devilina. These three men were also, with others, founders of a club called The Working Terrier Club in the fifties. Unfortunately this Club fizzled out quite soon.

Mrs. Leatt had a very famous and very strong kennel of top winning Borders. These were shown fearlessly in variety classes and did sterling work in helping judges to recognise that the Border could win top honours in variety competition: the Leatty Borders were sound, well presented and showed themselves off well. The first of the many Champions was Ch. Leatty Lace (Bladnoch Brock of Deerstone ex Leatty Sadie)—this bitch came down the tail female from Ch. Brimball of Bridgesollers and was born in 1947, winning her title in 1949. Then came a famous stud dog of his day, Ch. Leatty Druridge Dazzler, sire of three Champions, and Ch. Lily of The Valley who won her two final C.C.s here. Ch. Leatty Lace mated to Ch. Future Fame bred Leatty Lass, the dam of Ch. Leatty Lucky, a blue and tan sired by Dazzler. Ch. Lily of The Valley and Ch. Leatty Lucky were exported eventually. Another blue and tan of note sired by Dazzler was Ch. Dryburn Dazzler who won his first C.C. from this kennel before returning to Miss Vaux. At eight years old, Lace was mated to Dazzler and bred Ch. Leatty Loyallass, a very sound bitch and smart. Ch. Braw Boy and Ch. Golden Imperialist both completed their titles under this management, and were both eventually exported to Holland. Ch. Leatty Billy Bunter was also made up here—and of course we bought our Ch. Leatty Juliet of Law from Mrs. Leatt. Ch. Jonty Lad came along to complete his title and he went to America. Ch. Leatty Joy Boy, bred by Mrs. Sullivan was made up winning his C.C.s in 1960. Then came Ch. Leatty Plough Boy who was made up in 1965, and Ch. Felldyke Badger who won his last two C.C.s from this kennel. Then came a great

character and favourite of the Leatts, Ch. Leatty Emblewest Betsy, bred by Miss Bolton, who was also made up
in 1965. Betsy and Plough Boy were firm favourites and
both lived with the Leatts to ripe old ages. Ch. Leatty
Felldyke Gorse won his first C.C. in the Leatts' ownership,
then went to Mr. Norman Cowgill, who made him up in
1968. Norman Cowgill it was who handled Mrs. Leatt's
dogs to many of their triumphs, when Mr. Leatt was too
busily engaged judging to handle them. So many other
famous Borders passed through this kennel, and a great
deal of pleasure has been given by these dogs, not only
to the Leatts, but to previous owners and breeders who
perhaps could not get to enough shows to do their dogs
justice, but were proud to see them make the grade with
the Leatts, and also to many people who purchased
foundation and show stock on the Leatts' advice and were
not disappointed. A great many good working Borders
came from the Leatts.

Another person to really push the Border into the
limelight at variety shows was Mr. Robert Hall. Again,
the dogs were smartly presented and handled, and shown
fearlessly to win many Best In Show awards, and these
people are the ones we must thank when we can win in
variety and group competition nowadays. They must have
taken bitter disappointments as well as the success.
Mr. Hall was an exhibitor of gundogs before the war, so
came into Borders with a knowledge of dogs and breeding.
With this benefit, he made a careful selection of bloodlines for foundation stock, which payed rich rewards
later. This kennel laid the foundation on the Bladnoch
line, which produced so many good strains. Deerstone
Mischief was born in 1943, by Callum out of Bladnoch
Patty, and she, mated to Devonside Diversion, bred
Deerstone Defender, a lovely dog who won the first C.C.
for Mr. Hall in 1947. Then Mr. Hall purchased the blue
and tan dog, Bladnoch Brock of Deerstone who sired
Ch. Leatty Lace, and Bladnoch Tinker Bell, his litter
sister. From Miss Garnett Orme he had two brood bitches:
on loan, Raisgill Rosa whose daughter by Ch. Aldham

Joker was Deerstone Ornesta, born 1943; and about ten years later, Raisgill Radella of Deerstone. Ornesta and Callum bred Deerstone Dauntless who sired Ch. Portholme Manly Boy, Defender sired Ribbleside Roger and also Skirden Serena, the dam of Ch. Portholme Manly Boy. Mr. Hall bred Ch. Deerstone Driver from Bladnoch Tinker Bell by Fearsome Fellow. He also bought Ch. Portholme Marthe of Deerstone, and did some good winning with her. However, domestic worries prevented Mr. Hall from continuing to show Marthe and Driver, so they were sold to Mrs. B. S. T. Holmes as foundation stock, along with Deerstone Dancer with whom Mrs. Holmes gained a Working Certificate. Both Driver and Marthe became Champions in 1951, and Marthe went on to win six C.C.s. Mated together they bred Ch. Wharfholm Winnie. At this time Mr. Hall was out of the show-ring for some time. Purchasing Raisgill Radella of Deerstone, and mating her to Ch. Portholme Manly Boy, who contained both Defender and Dauntless, Mr. Hall bred that great dog Ch. Deerstone Destiny. He won twelve C.C.s and for many years held the post-war record in the breed. Destiny knew he was great and had the deportment and behaviour of a king. He sired Ch. Harranby Wanda and Harranby Dai, and out of Deerstone Grizella (an outcross bitch) Ch. Deerstone Realization, winner of five C.C.s in 1961, Deerstone Tinkerbell, winner of one C.C. also in 1961, and Deerstone Masterpiece. Ch. Realization sired Ch. Rhosmerholme Aristocrat (out of a Tinkerbell granddaughter) and the C.C. winners · Happy Chance of Welgrim, Chevinor Rascelle, Corburn Ottercops Farm Lad and Hanleycastle Julie, and was grandsire to Ch. Wharfolm Warrant, Ch. Maid of Honour and Ch. Chevinor Rasamat. A mating of a half-brother and -sister, both by Masterpiece, produced Ch. Benthor Garry. The mating that gave Ch. Deerstone Destiny was repeated and gave Ch. Deerstone Desirable, but to Mr. Hall's disappointment she did not breed on. By mating Tinkerbell to Klein Otti (a Ch. Billy Boy son and therefore tracing back through

Callum to the Bladnoch blood), Mr. Hall bred four very important Borders: Ch. Deerstone Delia, Ch. Deerstone Debrett, Rhosmerholme Deerstone Damien (sire of Ch. Rhosmerholme Recruit and Ch. Mansergh Rhosmerholme Amethyst) and Deerstone Deborah (dam of Ch. Bounty Tanner). From Mr. W. Hooton came Ch. Browside Rip of Deerstone, who contained the blood of Dauntless, Driver and Marthe, and her daughter by Ch. Realization, Deerstone Judy. Both proved to be super brood bitches, as their many descendants prove. Judy to Ch. Portholme Macsleap bred another great dog, Ch. Deerstone Douglas, and his sister Deerstone Decorative, the dam of Ch. Gatehill Copper Nob. Douglas was owned in partnership with Miss Bland, with whom he lived, and as a result was not heavily campaigned in the ring where he won seven C.C.s, nor was he used more than once or twice at stud—rather a loss to the breed. Ch. Rip and Ch. Destiny bred the C.C. winning Deerstone Dalesman, Deerstone Duskie (sire of Ch. Deerstone Busybody Madam) and Deerstone Delight (dam of Solway Cawfields Duke, who sired Ch. Eignwye Tweed and Ch. Workmore Rascal). Two Champions to descend from Bladnoch Brock of Deerstone, apart from the Ch. Leatty Lace family, were Ch. Eardiston Fettle and Ch. Eignwye Enchantress, through Brock's daughter Deerstone Dill, the mother of Eardiston Sailor who sired Ch. Fettle and the mother of Enchantress. As Tweed also descended from Enchantress, he contained that line as well as the Rip line. To Ch. Deerstone Debrett, Rip produced Deerstone Daybreak, the dam of three Champions bred by Mr. Ellis Mawson including Ch. Deerstone Falcliff Ramona. Judy mated to Ch. Portholme Mr. Moses bred Ch. Deerstone Dugmore (sire of Ch. Hobbykirk Destiny and the C.C. winning Tylview Butcher Boy, who sired Rhosmerholme Capacious), Deerstone Dugmal, a working certificate holder who sired Ch. Deerstone Larkbarrow Rainbow, and Deerstone Dugmerle, the dam of Eignwye Elvira, two C.C.s. Rainbow's dam, Deerstone Dimity, was by Ch. Portholme Mr. Moses out of Ch. Deerstone Delia. Apart from the many Deerstone descendants in the ring today, there are many overseas bearing titles. Ch. Debrett was exported to America, and Ch. Dugmore to Germany.

Within a few miles of Mr. Hall and the Deerstones live Mr. Duxbury and the Ribbleside Borders, which appear again behind so many winners. A very modest man and a well respected judge, Mr. Duxbury has had a lovely type of Border as long as I have known him, and no doubt for many years before that, when I was still in nappies! Mr. Duxbury's father was a breeder of Terriers, so Mr. Duxbury knew what he was about as soon as he started breeding Borders. What an advantage this is, as the knowledge acquired growing up with dog breeders cuts out the mistakes and false starts made by raw novices. Deerstone Dainty (Devonside Diversion ex a Callum-Bladnoch bitch) appears to have been the foundation, and she, mated to Ch. Swallowfield Garry bred Ribbleside Rusk. Rusk mated to Deerstone Defender bred Ribbleside Roger, and he sired Ch. Portholme Maire and Mamie and Ch. Portholme Mirth also descended from him. Another foundation was Ribbleside Risk, by Callum, and she was mated to Devonside Diversion, and produced Ribbleside Red Racquet, who, mated to Portholme Gaylass by Deerstone Dauntless, bred Ribbleside Rocket who sired Ch. Wharfholm Wench, Ch. Wharfholm Wizard and Ch. True Temper, from whom are descended several Champions. Rocket won the first C.C. for Mr. Duxbury in 1954. Another by Rocket was Browside Gypsy, the dam of Ch. Thrushington Georgie and Ch. Browside Rip of Deerstone. Steadily breeding on the same lines, Mr. Duxbury bred a lovely bitch, Ribbleside Recording Star who won two C.C.s in quick succession in 1965, but unfortunately died very soon afterwards, before she could either breed a litter or win her title. She descended from Ribbleside Mainstay, whose breeding reads Ch. Portholme Manly Boy—Ribbleside Red Racquet—Portholme Gaylass—Deerstone Dainty, thereby including all Mr. Duxbury's early breeding with his foundation stock. Mainstay also sired the dam of Ch. Cravendale Copper. A great-great-grandson of Rocket, Ch. Ribbleside Falcliff Trident, became Mr. Duxbury's first Champion and won eight C.C.s for good measure. Mr. Duxbury had another bitch line in Ribbleside Rhapsody, a daughter of Ch. Eardiston Fettle. Rhapsody mated to Kelin Otti bred Ribbleside Tagaroa, whose daughter Duttonlea Maria mated to Copper (from Mainstay) bred Ch. Duttonlea Mr. Softy, a dog with one of the best otter-heads I have yet to see. Ch. Trident sired Ch. Duttonlea Lillian out of Ribbleside Brockanburr Mandy, who was out of Ribbleside Regal Maid. A son of Trident, Ribbleside Ringman, onto a Tagaroa-Rocket descendant, bred Ch. Ribbleside Ridgeman, with which Mr. J. Lindley won two C.C.s and gained a working certificate. With Mr. Duxbury his total was brought to five C.C.s, of which four were won at Breed Club shows, and all of them under died-in-the-wool specialists. Ridgeman's puppies resemble him in type, and the first to win a C.C. is Mr. Bradley's bitch Ch. Gaelic Coffee. A descendant of the litter brother to Recording Star, is Wharfholm Mansergh Tinkerblue, again a good headed dog.

Mr. A. L. Waters of Hexham bred Ch. Billy Boy in 1949, by Callum ex a Ch. Boxer Boy daughter. This dog proved to be one of the best sires there has been in the breed, siring Mr. Waters' Ch. Hill Girl, Ch. Redbor Revojet, Ch. Braw Boy, Ch. Dipley Dinghy, Ch. Leatty Billy Bunter, Ch. Leatty Plough Boy, Ch. Full Toss, Ch. Silver Sal, Ch. Counden Trudy (dam of Ch. Counden Troena) and Ch. Winstonhall Counden Tim, as well as the famous sires Montime, Klein Otti and Northern Gleam. Montime sired Ch. Richies Dream (dam of Ch. Wharfholm Blue Moon and Ch. Wharfholm Wayward Wind, the dam of Ch. Wharfholm Wonderlad), her full sister Ch. Portholme March Belle, and their brother, Monsoon (sire of Ch. Mansergh April Mist, whose grand-daughter is Ch. Mansergh Barn Owl, and of Dandyhow

Siani from whom came Ch. Borderbrae Commodore and Ch. Borderbrae Candy). Northern Gleam sired Ch. Jimmy Trip. Klein Otti sired Ch. New Halfpenny, Ch. Felldyke Badger, Ch. Deerstone Debrett and Ch. Deerstone Delia. Also by Ch. Billy Boy was Mr. Walters' Kilmeny, two C.C.s, Harbottle, two C.C.s, Bell of The Ball, one C.C., Fellhouse Knapp (sire of Ch. Primrose who was the dam of Ch. Jonty Lad), one C.C., Regal Rusty, two C.C.s and Ludside Lanternhill Ilfracombe Mascot, one C.C.

The merging of the Ch. Future Fame and Ch. Billy Boy bloodlines bred Harbottle, Ch. Ringmaster, Kilmeny, Fellhouse Knapp, Ch. Leatty Billy Bunter, Regal Rusty, Klein Otti, Montime, Ch. Winstonhall Counden Tim, Ch. Counden Trudy, Daletyne Club Member, C.C., Ch. Sally Laurus, Ch. Mansergh Dandyhow Bracken, Ch. Kathyanga, and many others.

Here perhaps I should mention the wonderful brood bitch Lassiebelle, owned by Mr. S. Bell. Mated to Ch. Billy Boy she bred Ch. Braw Boy. To Ch. Billy Boy's son and her grandson, Montime, she bred Portholme Bellarina, dam of Ch. Portholme Matinee and granddam of Ch. Portholme My Fair Lady. To Ch. Future Fame she bred Jessabelle, owned by Mr. J. S. Newton. Jessabelle to Ch. Billy Boy bred Ch. Leatty Billy Bunter and Montime. By Overtime, Jessabelle bred Ch. Joytime. Daletyne Club Member was produced by mating a Montime son to a Ch. Joytime daughter, and Ch. Sally Laurus and Ch. Kathyanga were bred by mating Ch. Joytime with his own granddaughter. Ch. Mansergh April Mist was the result of mating a Montime son to a Ch. Joytime granddaughter. Portholme My Della, C.C. was from mating a Ch. Joytime son to a Montime daughter. Ch. Wharfholm Wayward Wind was from a Montime daughter mated to a grandson of both Montime and Ch. Joytime. Daletyne Rory, the noted sire, was bred on the same pattern as Ch. Kathyanga, Ch. April Mist and Co., only Montime and Joytime appear slightly further back. It is interesting to note that the tremendous influence of Jessabelle is through her sons.

Mr. Donald Goodsir's Carahall prefix appeared on some good Borders. By mating Caravicky, the founder of the strain, to Devonside Dignity he bred Carahall Crystal, and she and Ch. Portholme Manly Boy bred Ch. Carahall Cornet, a very typy dog. Miss Long used this dog on Winstonhall Whin, producing a blue and tan C.C. winner Winstonhall Wiseman, who was later owned by Mr. Goodsir, and another C.C. winning dog, Winstonhall Randale. Cornet sired Ch. Covington Dove, again of outstanding type, who eventually joined Mrs. Aspinwall's Farmway Borders. Winstonhall Wiseman sired Ch. Carahall Coffee. Caravicky was mated to a son of Deerstone Dauntless, Carahall Croney, and this bred Carahall Charm. Charm back to Cornet bred the C.C. winning Carahall Comrade and Carahall Coralyn. In 1962, Coralyn and Ch. Coffee produced Ch. Carahall Cicely and Ch. Gay Gordon, the latter sired Ch. Hawkesburn Beaver. Ch. Covington Dove was the granddam of Ch. Farmway Red Robin, and thus two of the leading stud dogs in the South descended from Ch. Cornet. Full sister to Ch. Cicely and Ch. Gay Gordon was W. Ronald Irving's Station Masher, who bred Ch. Arnton Fell. Yet another sister was Carahall Coke, the dam of Farmway Northern Piper, from whom descend Ch. Hobbykirk Destiny and Ch. Starcyl Bracken. There are many descendants of Ch. Hawkesburn Beaver and his son Ch. Handy Andy, so the Carahall line lives on.

Miss B. Eccles is a working enthusiast and very many of the terriers bearing the Chalkcroft prefix held Working Certificates. Apart from her tremendous knowledge and experience of the Border in the Hunting field, she also had considerable success in the show-ring in the late 1940s and '50s. Her first Champion was Ch. Fancy Girl of Chalkcroft, by Devonside Diversion out of Portholme Gypsy Maid, born 1946. This bitch with Dipley Dusty bred the C.C. winning Chalkcroft Duster. Then followed Chalkcroft Heiki, line bred to Callum, winner of two

C.C.s. Out of Dronfield Merrylegs, by Chalkcroft Duster, Miss Eccles bred Ch. Chalkcroft The Card, and also by Duster out of a similarly bred bitch, Ch. Chalkcroft Fancy. Ch. The Card sired Raisgill Romance, C.C. winner, and Heiki sired Grelund Chota, one C.C. The last dog to be seriously shown by Miss Eccles was the C.C. winner, Chalkcroft Puzzle, a really workmanlike and active terrier. He combined all the Chalkcroft blood. Miss Eccles has now abandoned the show-ring in favour of working her Borders. I suspect she has always valued their gameness above other attributes.

The Wharfholm prefix is known the world over and many lovely Borders have come from this kennel. Mrs. B. S. T. Holmes has always shown her dogs fearlessly in variety competition with considerable success, and the high standard she has kept has contributed to the recognition of the Border as a serious competitor at all levels of competition. The foundation stock were Ch. Portholme Marthe of Deerstone, Ch. Deerstone Driver and Deerstone Dancer. 1951 was a year to remember for Mrs. Holmes, as she made up both Marthe and Driver, Marthe eventually winning a total of six C.C.s. Mated together, they bred Ch. Wharfholm Winnie and the C.C. winning Leatty Wharfholm Wideawake, also in 1951—a busy year! Winnie also won six C.C.s. The next year Marthe went to Ribbleside Rocket and bred the litter brother and sister Champions Wharfholm Wizard and Wench. Both Dancer and Wench gained Working Certificates. Ch. Wizard and Ch. Winnie bred Ch. Wharfholm Wink, who gained a Working Certificate when owned by us at the age of five years plus. Another by Ch. Wizard was our Ch. Leatty Juliet of Law, who was out of a Wideawake daughter. She also gained a Working Certificate; her sister, Sporting Lady, was the dam of the C.C. winning Leatty Broadmoor Ben. Mrs. Holmes admires the blue and tan Border, and purchased Wharfholm Hallbourne Blue Bracelet from Mrs. Twist. Mated to Ch. Wizard, this produced Wharfholm Wishbone (dam of

84

C.C. winning Wharfholm Wrex by Portholme Mustard) and Ch. Mansergh Wharfholm Wistful. Bracelet to Ribbleside Mainstay bred Ch. Cravendale Copper's dam, Wharfholm Whip-it-Quick, a blue and tan, and Wharfholm Whimsical. From Mr. Morrison, Mrs. Holmes bought Ch. Wharfholm Blue Moon, who never bred, and later, her half sister, Ch. Wharfholm Wayward Wind. Ch. Wistful to Ch. Brookend Baggins (doubling on Ch. Hallbourne Blue Val) bred a blue and tan, Ch. Wharfholm Wizardry. A Wizard son, Wharfholm Harranby Topper, himself a C.C. winner, mated to Wharfholm Wistieslass (Wrex-Wistful) bred Ch. Mr. Tims and Wharfholm Mr. Wonderful. Wistieslass to Harranby Quest bred Ch. Wharfholm Warrant, later owned in partnership with Mr. G. E. Hutchinson. To date Ch. Warrant has sired Ch. Mansergh Barn Owl, Ch. Wharfholm Wonderlad (out of Ch. Wayward Wind), Ch. Final Honour and his litter sister Ch. Summer Belle, and the C.C. winners Yorkshire Life and Bannerdown Viscount. Ch. Final Honour has sired Ch. Step Ahead and the C.C. winning Oudenarde Simon Burn. From the litter sister of Ch. Mansergh Barn Owl has come the C.C. winning Rockinghamwood Tamara. Ch. Wizardy to Whimsieslass (Mr. Wonderful and Whimsical) bred the C.C. winning Wharfholm Top Hostess. Wizardy sired the lovely bitch Pia Annie Laurie, dam of Wharfholm Witchie, C.C. winner. Brookend Arwen joined the Wharfholms, as did the blue and tan, Wharfholm Mansergh Tinkerblue, these two both winning C.C.s.

Mr. and Mrs. Walter Gardner's Maxton strain is one of the few distinct strains remaining in the breed today, and has been bred with careful thought throughout the years. The first C.C. winner was Maxton Red Bell, by Ch. Future Fame out of a Tweedside Red Playboy bitch, in 1954. Out of her litter sister, Maxton Red Honey, by Grenor Max (whose pedigree is almost that of Ch. Future Fame in reverse order) he bred Ch. Maxton Mannequin, and out of Mannequin by Ch. Bargower Silver Dollar (which Mr. Gardner discovered on a farm and handled to his title in six weeks) he bred Ch. Maxton Miss Mink, a bitch I admired greatly. Another sister to Red Bell and Red Honey was Maxton Red Princess, who mated back to Ch. Future Fame bred Maxton May Queen, and she in turn put back to Ch. Future Fame, bred Ch. Maxton Matchless. Ch. Matchless to Tresta (Ch. Girvanside Cruggleton Don—Ch. Girvanside Tigress Mischief) gave two very famous Borders. First, that great show bitch, Ch. Marrburn Morag, owned by Mrs. McKnight, and secondly the well known worker with the Dumfries Otterhounds, Millbank Tarka. Ch. Morag, to Ch. Happy Day bred Ch. Starrburn Merrymaid and to her own sire, Ch. Matchless, bred Ch. Maxton Monarch, Ch. Starrburn Sultan and Maxton Mhairi. Mhairi mated back to Millbank Tarka bred Ch. Maxton Marla, Ch. Maxton Makrino and Starrburn Maxton Marina, winner of two C.C.s. Another by Millbank Tarka, and like his father a legend in his lifetime as a fearless worker, was Oxcroft Rocket, C.C. winner and sire of Ch. Oxcroft Vixen, and out of his own daughter who was also a granddaughter of Matchless, sire of Ch. Oxcroft Moonmagic, six C.C.s. and sire of Ch. Sundalgo Salvador and Ch. Sundalgo Serenade. Maxton Moonraker, a daughter of Red Honey, founded the Foxhill strain.

Mr. and Mrs. Benson started without a prefix. Ch. Joytime was their first Champion, made up in 1956 and winner of five C.C.s. He sired Ch. Kathyanga, Ch. Sally Laurus and Ch. Leatty Felldyke Gorse, as well as the C.C. winners Kennelworth and Joygirl owned by the Bensons, and Sun Saga and Pride of Bothal. Ch. Joytime was a daughter of the famous Jessabelle. Monsoon was purchased, and to Joygirl bred Daletyne Club Member, C.C. winner. Monsoon also came from the Lassiebelle strain. There was some interchange of stock with the Dandyhow kennel, Kennelworth went to Dandyhow, and the C.C. winning Dandyhow Belle Sibelle came to Daletyne, along with Dandyhow Bonnie Scot. Joygirl to Bonnie Scot bred the C.C. winning Daletyne Valentine and Ch. Eignwye Daletyne Santara. Belle Sibelle to Club Member bred Daletyne Delight, C.C. winner. Dandyhow Beautiful Susan also came, and to Monsoon bred Daletyne Solitaire. Bonny Scot and Joygirl bred Belletime, who to Dandyhow Brussel Sprout bred Daletyne Minstrel. Solitaire and Minstrel bred a sire of merit in Daletyne Rory. Out of a descendant of Monsoon and Belletime, Rory sired Ch. Daletyne Dundrum, and the C.C. winning Daletyne Cinderella. Rory and Belle Sibelle bred Ch. Highland Gyp sire of Ch. Corburn Corn Dolly, the ill-fated C.C. winner Cyron Carona, and Foxhill Fabulous, the dam of three Champions. Rory and Valentine really produced the "goods", Ch. Daletyne Decora, Ch. Daletyne Batchelor, the C.C. winning Daletyne Dubonnet, Daletyne Digger (dam of Ch. Oxcroft Vixen) and Daletyne Druidess (dam of Ch. Lady Lucinda and Ch. Lucky Lucy) were all the result of this. Ch. Batchelor sired Ch. Motcombe Rossut Barnbrack. Kennelworth and Belle Sibelle bred Daletyne Vixen, dam of Ch. Felldyke Badger and granddam of Ch. Leatty Felldyke Gorse. Daletyne Solitaire to a Bonny Scot-Joygirl daughter bred Daletyne Magic, dam of Oxcroft Rocket. Daletyne Richie, a Monsoon son, sired Ch. Wharfholm Wayward Wind, and Monsoon sired Ch. Mansergh April Mist and Dandyhow Siani. Daletyne Antara was a Ch. Joytime son, he appears behind Ch. Llanishen Illse of Clipstone, Ch. Llanishen Penelope and Ch. Temeside Joss. It is really impossible to list all the descendants of the Daletynes as there are a huge number in the ring at this time.

Mr. R. Morrison has been remarkably successful as a breeder, breeding Ch. Richies Dream, Ch. Wharfholm Wayward Wind, Ch. Portholme March Belle, Ch. Leatty Ploughboy and Monsoon, all from the line of his good bitch, Xmas Box.

Without any shadow of doubt, Mrs. Sullivan's Dandyhow prefix will live for ever as one of the greatest in the breed. She was brought up amongst Border Terriers, and has always had them in the family. However, the foundation of the Dandyhow strain was not laid until she bought two bitches, both born in 1950.

One of these was Bint Superior, by Ch. Swallowfield Garry out of Dronfield Vixen. The other was Brin's Selection, by Ch. Tweedside Red Playboy out of Firefly.

The first litter bred was from Bint Superior by Ch. Future Fame; one of these puppies was Cobber, who mated to Brin's Selection bred Beautiful Spy, an important brood bitch here, and Jemima Lass, the dam of Ch. Primrose.

Beautiful Spy mated to Greenbriar bred Wallacrag Wendy (dam of Ch. Dandyhow Bitter Shandy), Bad Sinbad and Brave Soldier.

The first Champion bred by Mrs. Sullivan was Ch. Leatty Joy Boy, by mating Bad Sinbad to Cobette, a daughter of Beautiful Spy by a Ch. Future Fame son, and another of this breeding was Dandyhow Bette's Survivor.

The first Champion made up by Mrs. Sullivan was Ch. Dandyhow Bitter Shandy, bred by mating Wallacrag Wendy to Fighting Fettle (Ch. Portholme Manly Boy ex Final Flutter). Dandyhow Sarah, C.C. winner, and Dandyhow Blue Shadow were also of this breeding. Both Bitter Shandy and Sarah went to America. Blue Shadow sired Ch. Dandyhow Suntan out of Bette's Survivor (Suntan sired Ch. Workmore Brackon), and Ch. Dandyhow Sultana out of Cobette.

Cobette proved a remarkable brood bitch. Mated to Brave Soldier she bred the C.C. winning Dandyhow Belle Sibelle, dam of Ch. Highland Gyp, and Dandyhow Brown Sherry and Dandyhow Bonny Scot. Apart from being the dam of Ch. Leatty Joy Boy and Ch. Dandyhow Sultana, she also bred Ch. Dandyhow Soroya, herself the dam of four Champions.

Beautiful Spy to Fighting Fettle bred the breed's super stud dog, Dandyhow Brussel Sprout, and the bitch who did so much for the breed in Eire by winning Best In

Show at an all breeds Championship Show, Irish Ch. Dandyhow Becky Sharpe of Arcairn.

Brussel Sprout (pet name " Veg.") apart from winning a C.C. himself sired: Ch. Mansergh Dandyhow Bracken, Ch. Dandyhow Shady Lady, Ch. Dandyhow Sea Shell, Ch. Dandyhow Sweet Biscuit, Ch. Dandyhow Sandpiper, Ch. Dandyhow Shady Knight (24 C.C.s, the breed record holder), Ch. Corburn Ottercops Farm Lassie, Ch. Border-brae Candy, Ch. Thrushgill Dandyhow Silhouette, and Ch. Vandamere's Band of Gold.

Dandyhow Belle Sibelle, her full brother Dandyhow Bonny Scot and Dandyhow Beautiful Susan went to join the Daletyne kennel, and from them came Ch. Eignwye Daletyne Santara, Daletyne Rory and all his clan, and Ch. Highland Gyp. Kennelworth came from Daletyne to Dandyhow, and he sired Ch. Dandyhow Susette out of a daughter of Beautiful Spy (this time mated to Mr. Renton's Regal Rusty).

Dandyhow Brown Sherry mated back to Ch. Future Fame bred Dandyhow Seamus, one of the last sons of that famous dog and Dandyhow Sapphire. Seamus back to Cobette (five lines to Ch. Future Fame) bred Ch. Dandy-how Soroya.

Ch. Dandyhow Soroya holds a unique record in the breed by being the dam of four Champions. Mated to Brussel Sprout she bred the three Champion bitches, Dandyhow Shady Lady, Dandyhow Sea Shell and Thrush-gill Dandyhow Silhouette. Shady Lady went to America. Ch. Soroya to Ch. Shady Knight bred Ch. Dandyhow Burnished Silver and Dandyhow Bolshevik, sire of Ch. Ragus Dark Chocolate, Ragus Demon King, two C.C.s, Borderbrae Countess, two C.C.s and Dandyhow Napoleon. Brown Sherry to Kennelworth bred Dandyhow Baby Sham who to Brussel Sprout bred Hanleycastle Wee Willow, dam of Ch. Hanleycastle Judy, and Hanleycastle Warbler. Brown Sherry to Blue Shadow bred Dandyhow Sheba, the dam of Ch. Yak Bob, a noted winner and worker.

89

Apart from siring Ch. Soroya, Seamus also sired Dandyhow Samaritan who sired Ch. Bounty Tanner and Dandyhow Saracen. Saracen sired Ch. Borderbrae Commodore, the C.C. winning Borderbrae Crusader, Ch. Temeside Joss, and out of Clipstone Dandyhow Lady, (a full sister to Ch. Shady Lady), Ch. Clipstone Carrots and Ch. Clipstone Guardsman. Ch. Carrots to Napoleon bred Ch. Clipstone Cetchup, and Clipstone Corsican.

Dandyhow Solitaire (Bette's Survivor by Dandyhow Starling, a Monsoon—Dandyhow Sapphire son) bred the two famous twins Ch. Dandyhow Shady Knight and Ch. Dandyhow Sandpiper by Brussel Sprout. Then to Ch. Cravendale Copper she produced Ch. Dandyhow Marjorie Daw.

Solitaire mated to Seascout, a Ch. Seashell daughter, bred Sweet Sherry, and she to Brussel Sprout bred the C.C. winning Dandyhow Bitter Lemon, the foundation of the Ragus kennel. Bitter Lemon to Bolshevik bred Ch. Ragus Dark Chocolate and Ragus Demon King, two C.C.s to date. Dark Chocolate onto a Ch. Commodore and Ch. Burnished Silver bitch, Dandyhow Wood Sorrel, bred Ch. Ragus Warlock.

A full sister to Starling, Dandyhow Siani, also proved a good brood bitch for Mr. Harold Roper. Apart from winning a C.C. herself, she bred Ch. Borderbrae Commodore and the C.C. winning Crusader, to Dandyhow Saracen; to Brussel Sprout she bred Ch. Borderbrae Candy, and Ch. Candy and Bolshevik bred Borderbrae Countess, two C.C.s. Ch. Borderbrae Commodore joined the Dandyhow string and completed his title there.

Ch. Dandyhow Shady Knight has been a wonderful representative of the Breed. Firstly as a showdog, breaking the record for C.C.s in the Breed by winning 24 under 24 different judges, over a period of five years, the first one being won when he was just over the year. He was the first Border ever to win a Terrier Group in the United Kingdom, which he did at Peterborough Championship Show on July 22nd 1971, under Mr. Walter Bradshaw, a great day of celebration for the Border world, who could rejoice that this had been achieved by a truly worthy specimen. Knight has proved that he deserved his wins by siring some really lovely stock, and he stamps these with his own special something that made him just that bit superior to other Champions. To date his puppies include Ch. Dandyhow Burnished Silver, Ch. Foxhill Foenix and Ch. Foxhill Fidelity, Ch. Hawkesburn Nutmeg, Ch. Llanishen Illse of Clipstone, Ch. Dandyhow Quality Street (out of a Daletyne Rory bitch), Ch. Vandamere's Burnished Gold, Ch. Oxcroft Pearl of Mansergh, the full brothers Ch. Dandyhow Spectator and Ch. Dandyhow Nightcap and also Dandyhow Bolshevik and Swedish Ch. Llanishen Ivanhoe (the sire of Ch. Llanishen Penelope). With others still to follow he could well beat Brussel Sprout's record as a sire—he has not been used as much as Brussel Sprout, simply because there were so many bitches by "Veg", and of course, Knight being by "Veg", meant this was rather too close to breed. Shady Knight and Burnished Silver were both the most attractive very dark grizzle when young, with jet black muzzle and ears. I remember them winning a huge Any Variety Brace class in the Waverley Market where they looked a picture.

Another here who has proved to be a successful sire is Dandyhow Napoleon. By Bolshevik out of a Shady Knight daughter, Dandyhow Blue Belle, he has sired so far Ch. Starcyl Bracken, Ch. May Isle Misty, Ch. Clipstone Cetchup, winner of three C.C.s whilst a puppy, and the C.C. winner Kenstaff Melanie.

Chevinor Dandyhow Sunsprite, a daughter of Brussel Sprout and Ch. Susette, mated to a son of Satin (sister to Seamus) bred Ch. Chevinor Rasamat, sire of Ch. Llanishen Rosemary of Counden.

The Dandyhow strain has provided a sure foundation for many kennels. A prolific strain, which appeared at a time when Borders were not breeding too freely, they were a source of good stock from which one could produce litters and therefore breed on from there. The Daletyne Hanleycastle, Borderbrae, Clipstone, Chevinor and Ragus kennels have all benefited by using the blood-lines intelligently. No doubt there will be many more Champions to come from the Bint Superior and Brin's Selection base.

Two other 'outsiders', apart from Kennelworth, Ch. Borderbrae Commodore and Ragus Demon King joined the Dandyhow team. Ch. Cravendale Copper spent his old age at Dandyhow, and left some good progeny, the first of whom to win a C.C. is the beautiful headed bitch Ch. Dandyhow Marjorie Daw. Vandameres Sunshine Souvenier was also bought in, containing basically Dandyhow and Daletyne breeding, and soon won her first C.C. but met an untimely end.

Another very well known strain is the Eignwye line of Mr. R. A. Williams of Hereford. He started with Raisgill Rainbow, and from her bred Eignwye Echo, his first C.C. winner, bred in 1951. From Eardiston Sally and Carry On, he bred the lovely Ch. Eignwye Enchantress, winner of six C.C.s. Then came Ch. Eignwye Daletyne Santara, with which he won four C.C.s, an outcross line. The purchase of Solway Cawfields Duke brought back a line carrying Ch. Enchantress, and put onto Eignwye Queen Beaver, bred by Mr. Renton, this produced Ch. Eignwye Tweed, a very typy dog who most unfortunately proved to be sterile—a bitter blow. A repeat mating produced the C.C. winner Eignwye High Society, who unfortunately was run over before she had time to win her title or, more important, to breed a litter. However, Duke onto Deerstone Dugmerle, bred a lovely bitch, Eignwye Elvira, winner of two C.C.s to date. Another of the same lovely type sired by Duke also is Ch. Workmore Rascal, dam of Ch. Workmore Waggoner.

Mr. Ellis Mawson's first Champion was Ch. Cravendale Chanter, a son of Ch. Hepple out of a Ch. Leatty Druridge Dazzler—Ch. Deerstone Driver bitch. He was made up in 1958. His daughter, Falcon Jewel to Hugill Ruffian, bred Falcliff Charmer, and she put back to Ch.

9   Ch. Mansergh April Mist—A wonderful
character and great favourite.

10   A granddaughter of April Mist,
Ch. Mansergh Barn Owl (centre) with her two
daughters Mansergh Muffet and Mansergh Muffin.

11   Borders running with the Border Foxhounds near Otterburn
      in 1973. The breed, previously known as the Coquetdale
      Terrier, took the name Border Terrier around 1880 because
      of its long association with the Border Foxhounds.

12   Tom Harrison, huntsman of the Kendal and District
      Otterhounds, photographed with three of his Borders
      on the river Eden near Appleby.

13   The steep country which the Border was bred to traverse following a horse. Note the racey build of the hounds.

14   Listening for the terrier underground. The man to the right of the sheepdog has his ear to the ground above the spot where the terrier will be.

15 "Nellie, Favourite of E. G. Paley" painted by
R. G. Brown in 1855. The breed of Nellie is
not known, but she obviously resembles an early
Border or an early Dandie Dinmont, of the time
when the breeds were more alike.

16 Mr. J. T. Dodd's Flint (1894) and his daughter Fury (1895).
Flint won more prizes than any other Border up to that time.

Chanter bred Ch. Falcliff Topper, winner of seven C.C.s and sire of five Champions. These were Ch. Cravendale Copper (owned by Mr. Mawson who made him up, then by Mr. Wrigley and finally by Mrs. Sullivan) out of Wharfholm Whip-it-Quick, Ch. Yak Bob out of Dandyhow Sheba, and, out of Deerstone Daybreak, Ch. Falcliff Tantaliser (exported to America), Ch. Ribbleside Falcliff Trident, eight C.C.s, and Ch. Deerstone Falcliff Ramona. Ch. Cravendale Copper sired Ch. Duttonlea Mr. Softy and Ch. Dandyhow Marjorie Daw; Ch. Trident sired Ch. Duttonlea Lillian; Ch. Tantaliser, out of a Charmer daughter, bred Chevinor Falcliff Traveller winner of one C.C.

Klein Otti and Mr. Searle, both great characters, are thought of together. Klein Otti appears close behind the breeding of many Champions, apart from his children Ch. Deerstone Delia, Ch. Deerstone Debrett, Ch. New Halfpenny and Ch. Felldyke Badger. Mr. Searle bought Swift and Sure from Mr. Adam Forster, won a C.C. with her, and she, mated to Klein Otti, bred the C.C. winners Sunday Special and Sun Saga. Sun Saga, back to her grandfather, Ch. Joytime, bred Ch. Sally Laurus and Ch. Kathyanga. Other important descendants of Klein Otti include Ch. Mansergh Dandyhow Bracken, Ch. Rhosmerholme Recruit, Ch. Deerstone Busybody Madam, Ch. Leatty Felldyke Gorse, Ch. Bounty Tanner, Ch. Foxhill Fusilier, Ch. Dandyhow Sweet Biscuit, Ch. Mansergh Rhosmerholme Amethyst, Ch. Borderbrae Commodore, Ch. Duttonlea Mr. Softy, Ch. Ribbleside Falcliff Trident and many, many more. Klein Otti was especially noted for his head and eye, which he passed on for generations, a very otter-like head and eye.

Another tremendous character is Mr. Jim Reid, a great sportsman and one who knows what the Border was for — none of your pretty pussy-faced ones here. Maybe he will be forgiving if I say that I always imagine the character Piper Allen to be not unlike Mr. Reid. I am sure his company would have been as entertaining, and his terriers as "likely". Many top Borders have passed through Mr. Reid's hands. One tough little dog was Mrs. Nixon's Fellhouse Knapp which Mr. Reid showed to win the C.C. at Ayr, and to be called into the short list in the Terrier Group, long before it was the fashionable thing to pull in the Border Terrier. By this dog, Mrs. Nixon bred Mr. Reid's Ch. Primrose, and from her Mr. Reid bred Ch. Jonty Lad, later exported to America. This dog is behind the Rhosmerholme bloodlines. Times are dull now that Mr. Reid does not show at Championship Shows—it seems ages since anyone danced the Northumberland sword dance in the ring, or cheered the winner of the working class with a ringing holloa.

Mr. and Mrs. Miller have bred with forethought and careful consideration one of the few true strains remaining, the Foxhills. The foundation was Maxton Moonraker, and putting her to Ch. Maxton Matchless they bred Foxhill Fantasy, who, mated to Portholme Mustard, bred their first C. C. winner, and a lovely Border she was too, Foxhill Fascination. Most unfortunately this bitch died before she could be made up, very bad luck for the Millers, who were comparative beginners at that time. Moonraker to Ch. Happy Day bred Foxhill Frangipani, and she mated to a Fantasy granddaughter bred Ch. Foxhill Fusilier. Another daughter of Fantasy, this time by Tweedside Red Ivor, bred Foxhill Flirt, and she to Ch. Happy Day produced Ch. Foxhill Firm Favourite. Maxton Moonraker was also mated to Ch. Happy Day and this gave Foxhill Fiery Flame. A granddaughter of his by Ch. Highland Gyp was bought in, Foxhill Fabulous, who proved to be one of those great brood bitches giving three Champion progeny. Mated to Ch. Fusilier, she bred Ch. Foxhill Fulbert, carrying three lines to Moonraker. This dog later went to the Bombax kennel in Sweden. Fabulous was then mated twice to Ch. Dandyhow Shady Knight, and bred Ch. Foxhill Foenix in the first litter, and Ch. Foxhill Fidelity in the second. I had the pleasure of giving a C.C. to both these beautiful bitches, and I often wonder which was the better of the two, it would be a very close contest. Ch. Fusilier and Ch. Foenix produced the bitch, to date holder of one C.C., Foxhill Foxglove, again carying three lines to Moonraker.

Another steady breeder has been Mrs. Marchant and her Hawkesburn prefix. Ch. Hawkesburn Beaver was her first Champion, a well known worker too; he held a Working Certificate and many scars to prove it. He sired Ch. Handy Andy and Ch. Hawkesburn Happy Returns out of Mr. Renton's Border Queen. Handy Andy sired Ch. Lucky Lucy, Ch. Lady Lucinda (granddam of Ch. Thoraldby Miss Mandy) and Ch. Elandmead Ragamuffin. Others by Beaver included Workmore Queenie (dam of Ch. Workmore Rascal), Cawfields Ballerina, (dam of Ch. Clipstone Hanleycastle Bramble) and Eignwye Queen Beaver, (dam of Ch. Eignwye Tweed).

Ch. Happy Returns mated to a grandson of Beaver, Hawkesburn Buffalo, bred Hawkesburn Merry Capers, a C.C. winner and foundation for Miss Churchill's Campanologia Borders. Another to lay a foundation from Merry Capers was Mrs. Hamilton and her Oudenarde Borders, breeding Oudenarde Simonburn, C.C. winner, in her first litter from a daughter of Merry Capers. Ch. Happy Returns was then mated to Ch. Dandyhow Shady Knight and bred Ch. Hawkesburn Nutmeg. To Ch. Shady Knight's litter-brother, Ch. Dandyhow Sandpiper, she bred another good bitch in Ch. Hawkesburn Spindle. Mrs. Marchant produces a very true type of Border, which are very game too.

Mr. Roper with his Borderbrae Borders is a well known figure at the northern shows. He showed Borders for many years, Eskview Outlaw and Borderbrae Bellman being well known winners in variety as well as breed shows. Purchasing Dandyhow Siani proved to be a wise move. Mated to Dandyhow Saracen she bred Ch. Borderbrae Commodore and his C.C. winning brother, Borderbrae Crusader. Next, Siani went to Dandyhow Brussel

Sprout, and bred the good bitch, Ch. Borderbrae Candy. She to Dandyhow Bolshevik bred Borderbrae Countess, holder to date of two C.C.s. Mr. Roper himself must hold a record in the breed, having won a C.C. at the Border Terrier Club Championship Show, the ambition of us all, on five consecutive years with Candy, 1971 and 1975, Crusader, 1972, and Countess in 1973 and 1974. An important descendant of Ch. Crusader is Ch. Ragus Warlock.

Mr. Roger Clements is a great supporter of the Working Border. His well known worker and show dog, Hanleycastle Russ is behind many winners and even more workers. He sired Ch. Hanleycastle Judy, a regular competitor in the working class, and her brother, Hanleycastle Jasper, sire of Ch. Clipstone Hanleycastle Bramble which Mr. Clements bred from a Ch. Hawkesburn Beaver daughter. The mother of Judy and Jasper, Hanleycastle Wee Willow, by Dandyhow Brussel Sprout, also bred Hanleycastle Warbler, the dam of Ch. Llanishen Illse of Clipstone, and granddam of Ch. Llanishen Penelope. Other C.C. winners descending from Russ are Brookend Arwen, Hanleycastle Julie, Bonnie Berrie and Ch. Temeside Joss. Dandyhow Saracen joined the Hanleycastle team as a stud dog.

Mr. Dennis Wiseman is another keen working Border enthusiast, and, like Mr. Clements, pays particular attention to temperament. This being the first essential of a working terrier it is all-important to these two breeders. His first C.C. winner was Hanleycastle Julie. He bred the C.C. winner at the Border Terrier Club 1969, Bonny Berry, by Solway Cawfields Duke out of a daughter of his working dog, Daletyne Antara, with a Hanleycastle Russ granddaughter. Another descendant of Antara is Ch. Temeside Joss. Out of Hanleycastle Warbler (by Antara) mated to Ch. Dandyhow Shady Knight Mr. Wiseman bred Ch. Lanishen Illse of Clipstone and Swedish Ch. Llanishen Ivanhoe. From Dandyhow Streetgate Wendy and Ivanhoe (both by Ch. Shady Knight) he bred Ch. Llanishen Penelope. It was hard luck that at the time Mr. Wiseman had Illse, Ivanhoe and Penelope in his kennel, his health failed. However, I am sure that their success must have helped him on the road to recovery. By Ivanhoe came Coppinswell Dandy Boy, sire of Ch. Workmore Waggoner, and Llanishen Raffles, dam of Ch. Llanishen Rosemary of Counden.

Mrs. Edna Garnett's Rhosmerholme line has consistently produced top class stock. Her first bitch was Leatty Liza who to Ch. Leatty Joy Boy bred Lady of Ribblesdale. Lady to Ch. Jonty Lad bred Rhosmerholme Rip, a lovely type but a shade big, the ideal requirements of a brood bitch. She proved this to be true by producing Ch. Rhosmerholme Rip and Ch. Mansergh Rhosmerholme Amethyst to Mrs. Garnett's Rhosmerholme Deerstone Damien. Amethyst went to Sweden and founded a huge dynasty of Champions there. Her great grandson is the C.C. winning Mansergh Wharfholm Tinkerblue. Ch. Recruit to Ch. Deerstone Realization bred Ch. Rhosmerholme Aristocrat, who created a sensation by winning her title in eleven days—good going by any standards. To prove that she was no "eleven day wonder", she came out three years later to win her fourth C.C. Her sister, Rhosmerholme Augustine, mated to Ch. Duttonlea Mr. Softy, bred Rhosmerholme Berry, who won a C.C. at an early age, then had a long illness which spoilt her chances of completing her title. Avenger, a full brother to Augustine, mated to Berry bred Ch. Braestone Voyager and the C.C. winning Braestone Vindicator of Rhosmerholme.

The Clipstone prefix is definitely one to be reckoned with, and has had considerable success in recent years. The first C.C. winner was bred by Mr. and Mrs. Jackson in 1965, by Ch. Brookend Baggins out of their first Border, Henleygrove Happy Girl. Their first Champion was Ch. Clipstone Hanleycastle Bramble, later exported to America. A judicial move was the purchase of Clipstone Dandyhow Lady, sister to three Champion bitches, from Mrs. Sullivan. Mated to Dandyhow Saracen, she bred Ch. Clipstone Carrots and Ch. Clipstone Guardsman in one litter. Guardsman later joined the Bombax kennel in Sweden. The Jacksons were lucky enough to purchase the good bitch, Ch. Llanishen Illse of Clipstone from Mr. D. Wiseman and made her up very easily. Ch. Carrots bred the sensational Ch. Clipstone Cetchup, winner of three C.C.s whilst a puppy, and Corsican, C.C. winner. Illse & Guardsman bred Ch. Clipstone Comma.

No chapter on influence in the breed would be complete without a reference to Mr. Ted Hutchinson. A wizard at presenting and handling a Border, he has helped many people in the Breed to achieve their success, and his advice and encouragement has started many novices who have gone on to become well known breeders. The first Border with which he won a C.C. (although he had already had considerable success in several other breeds including Chihuahuas and Whippets) was Ch. Vic Merry, owned by Miss H. Vaux, for whom he also made up Ch. Dryburn Dazzler and Ch. Dryburn Devilina. For Mrs. H. P. Longworth he piloted Ch. Knavesmire Kopper, and for Mr. Ted Harper, Ch. Barnikin. Then came Ch. Maid of Honour, a Kopper daughter, for Mr. H. Jenner. In partnership with Mrs. Holmes he owns Ch. Wharfholm Warrant, and made him up. My own Ch. Barn Owl was bred by Mr. Hutchinson. For Mr. Jenner, and later owned in partnership with him, he made up the litter brother and sister, Ch. Final Honour and Ch. Summer Belle, by Warrant out of a Kopper bitch. These won both C.C.s at Crufts in 1973, and Ch. Final Honour went Reserve Best Terrier, a great honour, before embarking for America from the show. He left behind an outstanding son, out of Ch. Maid of Honour, namely Ch. Step Ahead. This dog delighted us all by winning the Terrier Group at Leicester Championship Show in 1974, on a Monday. On the Saturday following, he repeated this at Birmingham Championship Show, and completed the amazing hat trick one week later, at

Darlington Championship Show—a great lift for the breed. He also won the Terrier Group at the W.E.L.K.S. in 1975. His outstanding movement won him these honours. By winning his twenty-sixth C.C., under twenty-five judges, in 1976 Ch. Step Ahead took the breed record previously held by Ch. Dandyhow Shady Knight. His outstanding movement won him these honours. Countless other Borders have been steered to high wins by Ted Hutchinson, but these records speak more than a list a yard long of the great understanding this man has for the Border.

It would take much more time and space to list all the Borders who have reached the heights of success in the show ring, and their breeders and owners. I hope that I may be forgiven for not cataloguing them all—to own one good dog may be lucky, to own two a coincidence, after that it proves that either the person concerned has a good eye for a dog, or has cashed in on the clever breeding behind the ancestors of his dogs!

Several patterns occur in these pedigrees, one noticable one being the success of the classic granddaughter to grandsire mating; this was responsible for producing Ch. Osmond Braw Lad, Ch. Tweedside Red Biddy, Ch. Swallowfield Nutmeg, Ch. Maxton Matchless, Ch. Falcliff Topper and the litter sister Champions, Sally Laurus and Kathyanga.

Half-brother to half-sister matings are not usually considered desirable by expert breeders, however the fact that to date some twenty-three champion Borders have been produced by this method might disprove this theory.

Ch. May Isle Misty is the result of an unusual pattern of breeding. Both her parents were the result of half-brother and -sister matings, so that her four great-grandsires are all one and the same dog, Ch. Dandyhow Shady Knight.

The mother to son mating has so far produced only two champions, both bitches, whilst father to daughter has produced three champions, all dogs.

The four grandparents, Ch. Girvanside Cruggleton Don, Ch. Tweedside Red Glamorous, Ch. Future Fame and Ch. Scotch Mist appear on the pedigrees of Ch. Rab Roy, Ch. Brieryhill Gertrude, Ch. Bright Light, Ch. Barnikin and Ch. Happy Day.

Stud dogs stand more chance of producing an impressive list of famous progeny simply because they can be mated to scores of bitches of different strains in their lifetime, whereas a bitch probably has at the most five litters in her lifetime. This means the chances of her "throwing a six" are very much less. For instance, the great sire Dandyhow Brussel Sprout served some fifty bitches, and from these seven bitches produced his ten Champions—of course, a great number of his bitches bred good stock which although they did not actually become Champions, bred on to produce Champions.

Cobette, a noted brood bitch was mated to five dogs, as opposed to Brussel Sprout's fifty bitches, and from these produced a number of top winners and winner producers. She bred forty-five puppies in all. Mated to Brave Soldier she bred Dandyhow Belle Sibelle, (a C.C. winner and dam of a Champion), Dandyhow Bonny Scot, (sire of a Champion), Dandyhow Beautiful Susan and Dandyhow Brown Sherry, both of whom appear behind many Champions. To a full brother of Brave Soldier called Bad Sinbad she gave Ch. Leatty Joy Boy and Bette's Survivor, the dam of a Champion. To Dandyhow Blue Shadow she bred Ch. Dandyhow Sultana. In her last litter, put back to her own grandson, she bred the dam of four Champions, Ch. Dandyhow Soroya. A remarkable record for a brood bitch which causes one to wonder just what her record would have been had she been a male not a female.

I maintain that a bitch who breeds just one top class puppy in her lifetime has fulfilled her purpose, there have been several in the breed who have bred three Champions which is a remarkable feat.

One such bitch was Causey Bridget, mated to Revenge

she bred Ch. Happy Mood, Ch. Blister and Ch. Tod-hunter. Another remarkable bitch was Dinger Queen. Mated to Ch. Ranting Fury then to his son Why Not and finally to his grandson, Neil Gow, she bred Ch. MacMerry, Ch. Vic Merry and Ch. Scotch Mist. This was all the more astonishing as Dinger Queen was born in 1943 and produced Ch. Scotch Mist in 1954! Mrs. Holmes owned Ch. Portholme Marthe of Deerstone who gave three Champions to two dogs. Jean's Wendy owned by Miss Galbraith gave three Champions all to one dog, as did Mr. Mawson's Deerstone · Daybreak. Mrs. McKnight's great Ch. Marrburn Morag bred three Champions, two to her own sire. Mr. Morrison's Xmas Box gave two to a son of Ch. Billy Boy and one to Ch. Billy Boy himself. Mrs. Sullivan has been extremely fortunate to own three of these superb brood bitches: Cobette who bred three Champions by different dogs, although two of the dogs were brothers, Dandyhow Solitaire who bred three Champions by two dogs, and Ch. Dandyhow Soroya who gave three Champions by Brussel Sprout and one by his son, Shady Knight. Mr. and Mrs. Miller also own one of these gems, Foxhill Fabulous who bred Ch. Foxhill Fulbert to a Foxhill dog and Ch. Foenix and Ch. Fidelity by Ch. Shady Knight.

It is significant to note that most of the stock from these wonderful bitches have bred on—the only line which we seem to have lost being that from Jean's Wendy, two of her Champions were exported early in their lives.

At the end of the book are two pedigrees illustrating examples of line-breeding and in-breeding, both of which have proved successful. However, after searching for hours, I have had to abandon the idea of a pedigree showing a complete outcross throughout. This would indicate that indiscriminate breeding does not pay dividends, the benefits are reaped by carefully thought out breeding, which is what I have tried to explain in this chapter.

CHAPTER 6

Choice of Foundation Stock

Foundation stock, be it for show, breeding, work or as a pet, should be chosen with as much care as a marriage partner, as one has to live with it for the duration of it's life, and with it's descendants. Unless, of course one can harden one's heart and realizing one's mistake, scrap it and start again.

It is worth delaying the purchase to look around carefully, if possible visiting shows or terrier shows to see which dogs appeal for type and character. By referring back to the breeder of these, one can find out whether there are any of a similar sort available. Breeders and exhibitors are most helpful and will answer any questions. put to them politely, to the best of their ability. I emphasise the words "put to them politely" as it is quite extraordinary that the general public look upon anyone breeding dogs as sub-human, and the rudeness we receive is not always conducive to a helpful reply.

If wanting stock from which to breed, it is worth waiting until an older bitch becomes available instead of taking a gamble on a young puppy. As bad mouths are still a breeder's nightmare, most breeders will run on a couple of bitch puppies until their second teeth have come through. Obviously, should one of these come with an incorrect bite, it is not suitable as a brood bitch. Under no circumstances should one be tempted to breed from a bitch with an undershot mouth. However, very often both bitch puppies will have perfect bites, and then one will be for sale. Such a bitch will cost a little more

102

than an eight weeks old puppy but is well worth the extra money. She will have been well reared as a potential show prospect for the breeder, the teeth are there and correct, and one can see the shape of the puppy with more certainty at this age (five or six months). Also she will be ready to show in a few weeks instead of having the long wait from eight weeks to six months. Although she may be the second best from her litter, by going to a good breeder, the chances are that she will be better than the best from less experienced breeders' litters, and even her breeder may have "backed the wrong horse" of the two bitch puppies—it has been known to happen more than once.

Should such a bitch not be available, other alternatives are to purchase an adult and proven brood bitch; from whom may be bred one more litter (the snag to this being that then the adult bitch has to either occupy valuable space in the kennel for some years, or a kind home be found for her) or to purchase two bitch puppies and run them on oneself until they have teethed. The snag to this being that, of two youngsters growing up together, one always tends to be topdog and to keep the other rather in it's shadow. Also they can lead one another off the straight and narrow into naughty ways, or become too dependent upon each other to the exclusion of recognising the authority of their owner. A breeder soon overcomes this by seeing the danger signals and splitting them up into different kennels. It is important that a young animal's affections should become centered primarily on its owner, not another dog.

Whether for a showdog, work or pet, it is advisable to decide clearly which sex is preferred. The old myth that a dog is less trouble to manage than a bitch should fool no-one. Any animal is a potential pest and a tie and responsibility. While a bitch is interested in sex only twice a year, a dog never really puts it far out of his mind.

For my own preference, I would take a bitch every time as I love the more elegant lines, and the character.

For some reason I have been very unlucky with the dogs I have tried to keep.

No dog or bitch should be allowed to roam the neighbourhood unattended. The owner should know at all times exactly where the dog is, and the answer is it should either be at home or with the owner. Legally the owner is responsible for any accident to humans which the dog might cause, which could run into tens of thousands of pounds were a human to be badly injured. It is advisable to insure against this.

A dog may be preferred for work as a bitch may be in season or confined to the maternity ward in the autumn or spring. Both sexes make equally good workers.

Having decided upon the strain, sex and age, the time comes to actually choose the animal. For whatever purpose the dog is required, the two most important attributes are temperament and health. Whatever the age there should be no signs of either nerves, shyness or agressiveness, and of course any animal that is not in prime condition should not be offered for sale.

Seven or eight weeks is the best age to select a puppy as this is the time their shape will be similar to the finished product. Here I must stress that a puppy sitting at the back of the box, looking appealing, is feeling either nervous, ill, or shy and should be avoided, as should any that is seen to "stand over" it's little brothers and sisters, as this will probably become a fighter. Puppies should never be picked up without the permission of the breeder, as there is a right and a wrong way to do this, and should one be dropped it´ may be badly damaged. The correct way to hold a puppy is under one's arm against one's body for support; with the palm of the hand supporting the weight between the front legs, the two elbows being held-in between the thumb and first finger and little finger and fourth fingers respectively.

To examine a puppy I like to set it up in a show stance on a table at eye-level. I look for a strong, short muzzle, well-filled under the eyes even at this age, paying particular attention to the under jaw at this age. Should this be conspicuous or at all prominent when viewed either fullface or from the side, this puppy should be avoided as the jaw will probably become undershot. The jaws seem to grow at different rates, which is why a puppy's mouth may suddenly "go". Plenty of width across the skull, and between the eyes, and a flattish head when viewed in profile are wanted. Apple skulls should be avoided. Fairly lowset ears, small, V-shaped and not too heavy are desirable. The neck should be fairly long, the shoulders clean and well-laid. The placement of the shoulder can be measured at this age and the shoulders should not be the broadest point of the puppy. They will be thicker at eight weeks, comparatively, than on the finished dog, but any thick ridges of bone should be avoided. The legs should be straight and well boned at this age, with small feet. Firm elbows are important, which should not turn out when the weight of the pup is gently pulled, by taking the weight of the head under the chin in one's hand and swaying the puppy, from side to side. The backline should be level and strong, the couplings not too short, the tail set on level with the backline very short and thick, tapering to a definite point, without any kinks when the hand is run along it. Longish hindlegs, well bent stifles and low set hocks, at a right angle to the ground are all required. I look for freedom in the hindlegs, and like them to stand rather further back than the root of the tail. The hindquarters should not be narrow across the pelvis, and the hocks should turn neither in nor out—the test for elbows also tests this, viewed from the rear of course! At eight weeks the coat should be hard with an undercoat. A light stand-off frizz does not matter, provided there is a hard coat beneath this, as this is just the first puppy coat growing out. Fluffiness should be avoided as, though this may be appealing, it depicts a soft adult coat, which is a perfect pest in a showdog and provides no protection in a working dog.

Points to avoid are: pointed muzzles; snipey (weak) foreface; bandy legs; wide thick shoulders; tied in elbows (these look as if there is a tight elastic band holding them in under the body); short backs; roached backs; long, thin, kinky or curly tails; pop-eyes; apple skulls; light eyes; narrow hindquarters; thin, long flat feet; very light or very heavy bone; short legs; fluffy or single coats; prominent jaws; straight stifles; knuckling over knees; double jointed elephant-like hocks; eyes placed too close together.

Puppies differ from strain to strain in their development. Those from some strains are fully developed at six months of age whilst others may not finish growing until around the twelve month mark, and may not be fully developed until two and a half years of age. The latter are usually the better lasters, and do not coarsen as they grow older.

When choosing a puppy it is a great help to know whether it comes from a fast or slow maturing line. However, whatever the bloodline, the basic frame of the dog must be correct right from the start. By experience one learns whether a head will develop or not. Provided the eyes are not placed too close together, the skull is broad, and the muzzle feels strong and not too long, the head will usually develop with time, although there may be a long wait before it does.

Colour is a matter of personal preference. Generally speaking, it should be remembered that Borders grow lighter in colour with maturity. A blue and tan will be black and tan in the nest, a nearly black puppy will be a very dark grizzle, a rich brown will be a red, and a dark brown and tan will be a dark grizzle. Wheatens are born very light. However, it is difficult to prognosticate the final colour of a Border, which accounts for the difference often noticed between the colour recorded on a registration card and the animal as an adult. Any white patch on the chest will grow less, as the puppy grows around it. Also, as the grizzling comes through, this tends to merge in, so does not really matter, within reason. White on the feet does stay, and is not appreciated by a judge of the old school although there is nothing specific against this in the standard. It would be perverse to start with a handicap, therefore white toes are not really to be recommended, although I can think of one very good C.C. winner with a white toe—but this may have stopped ·him from winning the other two. Of course white toes make no difference to a worker.

For work, the most sensible-looking character, neither a retreating coward, nor visibily aggressive, should be selected. An inquisitive nature, but not foolhardy, such as the puppy who approaches the old scrubbing brush with caution, and then pounces and kills it once it has established what it is, not too short backed, a good length of neck and leg, scope and width in the hindquarters, no restrictions in conformation, and with good bone and feet, but of a middle range in size, would be the best bet. Although most Borders will work if the opportunity is correctly presented to them, there are some excellent working strains and it would be advisable to buy a puppy from known working stock. However, the fact that both parents are game and entered terriers, does not always mean that the puppy will work—there are occasional dogs which never take to work—one we bred from the best possible working parents, but one of the puppies was just to polite to work, despite the attempts of everyone. On the other hand, Ch. Wharfholm Wink, a five year old bitch who had never worked in her life, took to work as a duck to water with no persuasion needed. A good double coat and loose thick skin is also essential for a worker. Working on a cold wet winter's evening, in snow, in a water-filled drain, or just in that typically English steady drizzle, the dog will really need the full protection of this coat.

If selecting a bitch entirely as a brood bitch, the rather doggy type of bitch is the one to go for. These bitches have more type to stamp on their puppies, and also more bone and substance to pass on to them. They are usually roomy bitches, a little too much length of back does not go amiss on a brood bitch, neither does a build resembling a cow, without the cow hocks of course. These bitches can always be mated to stud dogs with rather more quality about them, but these are the ones that I would choose every time as a brood proposition, in preference to the more refined, quality type that might make a top show bitch.

For a pet, either a young puppy, or one of the two previously mentioned five-month old litter sisters would be just as good, depending on how much one wants to struggle with rearing a lively youngster in the home, However, there is a third choice here, which I recommend wholeheartedly, and that is the three or four year old ex-show dog or bitch, who has become redundant either through not quite making the top heights in the ring, or has retired having done his or her stint of breeding, which the breeder dearly would like to see settled in a comfortable, happy home. By enquiring around the breeders, these are found. As they are rather special dogs, they are not advertised for sale, as the breeders are always happy to keep them until the right home comes along. These are very civilized and often well-travelled dogs which take readily to family life and can give many years of companionship. These are usually house-trained, or if not that, by this age are very clean in their habits. It is most unusual to hear of one of these dogs "making mistakes" in the house.

Again I must stress that no ownership of any animal should be entered into without careful consideration and choice. The dog or bitch selected will be a companion for anything from ten to fifteen years, given ordinary luck, and like a marriage partner, cannot be returned and is extremely difficult to dispense with, if proved to be incompatible!

CHAPTER 7

Puppy and Kennel Management

The first day in its new home is most important to the new puppy or adult. It will be feeling very strange and lonely, but, being a Border, will reflect this by being very much on its dignity, probably sitting with its head turned away and presenting a stolid backview to its new owners.

An older dog should be kept on a tight collar and lead for the first few days. When I purchase an adult I keep it with me for the first two days and nights at all times. If I must leave it, I leave it in my bedroom in the travelling box in which it sleeps for the first few days. No trouble should be too much to secure the safety of the newcomer at this time, as the terror inspired should it escape and become lost in strange surroundings is virtually ineradicable, and a domesticated dog reverts to "wild dog" if living rough for only a few days. I shall never forget the primitive look in a Dachshund's eye who had been recaptured after living out for a week or so—the hidden instincts soon emerge.

When in the room with me, the new dog is tied to a table leg should I be preoccupied, but I talk to it constantly and take it for little walks and give it plenty of tasty titbits—anything to make it feel more at home. It is a rewarding moment indeed when one is honoured with the first little wag or lick, and from then the Border very soon settles. However, no risks should be taken at the early stages of re-habilitation.

The bed should be snug and comfortable, free from draughts. The change of environment, food, water and general emotional upheaval must be a shock to the system of any dog, however easy-going. It is equivalent to a child's first day at a new school, and I am sure everyone remembers that traumatic experience. The dog should be kept comfortable and dry for these first few days.

If possible, the main part of the diet should be altered as little as possible so that the stomach does not become upset. Should this happen, a stiffly made rice pudding will soon rectify the condition. A common mistake made in the enthusiasm of owning a new dog, is to give it a special treat, either in the form of a drink of milk, or a new owner has been known to purchase heart or liver, all of which can upset the digestive system.

Once entente cordiale has been established, with lots of tail-wagging and greeting, I allow the new girl to trail her lead around the house, calling her up to me for petting frequently. As soon as I am positive that she will allow me to catch her in the house, I dispense with the lead, indoors, but am still careful about "jailbreaks" through open doors.

Outside, I drop the lead for a short time on the walk, making sure that this is done in an enclosure of some sort so that all is not lost should the dog decide not to be caught again.

From then onwards the mutual trust is built up until the regular routine is established. The transition from house to kennel is made gradually and care is taken that the first hours in the kennel are not too long, so that the kennel is not looked upon as a place of punishment.

The young puppy will, also, require a warm, draught-proof bed. For the first night with me it sleeps in a shut travelling box with lots of bedding as then, however plaintive and heart-rending the cries (which there will be), I know the puppy is warm and in its bed. For those who did not see the classic film 'The Lady and The Tramp', let me say here and now, unless you intend to have a dog on your bed for ever, do not soften your heart to those cries the first night!

It is important that the puppy should be inoculated as soon as possible after it has settled. One should check the inoculations of an adult purchase too, for it is surprising how many are not inoculated, or are not up to date with their boosters. The breeder will advise which inoculation to have. Until this has been done, the dog or puppy should not be allowed onto 'doggy' ground where it can pick up infection.

Generally, Borders are very clean by nature and easily house-trained.

Provided that the puppy is taken out frequently, and especially after meals, it will soon become very house-proud. A scolding should a mistake occur will soon register.

Once the new dog has really settled it is a good idea to worm it but it should be safely over any upset caused by change of diet and water and of course well over any inoculations which it may have had. There is usually no urgent hurry for this to be done. Either a proprietary brand of roundworm pills from the chemist or a dose provided by the local Veterinary Surgeon may be used for this. The dog should be wormed regularly but not too frequently. This is particularly necessary should there be sheep in the district frequented by the dog.

Training to the degree of training required should be undertaken by the owner. However, every dog should be at least lead trained and taught that all-important command "no".

A puppy should be lead trained at about three months of age. A small puppy collar is needed, not too expensive as it soon grows out of this, or an adult collar cut-down and with a hole made with a meat skewer or knitting-needle, to fit sufficiently tightly so that the puppy cannot slip out backwards. Halter-breaking, as any other training, should be only undertaken on a day when all is well with the world and one is feeling fit, happy and well—otherwise the required patience may be rather lacking. A quiet

111

place, free from disturbance and distraction, should be chosen. The puppy is taken there, and then the collar and lead are put on, talking to the puppy all the while kindly. A firm hold is kept on the end of the lead. The puppy will lie spreadeagled and with eyes rolling. Still talking to it, a gentle tug is made on the lead, whilst walking forward with the command 'come on' in a kind tone of voice. Enticement in the form of favourite food will also work. The puppy will gradually move forward and walk with you, vocal encouragement should be given nonstop. At some stage there will be a tugging match resembling 'playing' a salmon on a fishing line. It is essential for the human to win this, so a firm grip should be kept on the end of the lead and the puppy must not be allowed to slip the collar. After trying all ways to escape, the puppy will probably adopt a position of surrender lying on the ground. It should now be encouraged to walk forward with you and once this is achieved the lesson should end, the collar being removed and a great fuss being made of the pupil. After a couple of days the lesson is repeated for a short time only. One should not overdo the training at any stage. I find that once the puppy is going well on its lead it likes to show off to the other dogs, so I take it and allow it to swank through the kennel bars on its lead. As soon as the puppy will walk with a swagger and without pulling back or fighting the lead it may go out for little walks.

Elementary training requires that the dog should walk on a lead without pulling. Apart from being extremely exhausting for those at either end of the lead, this can ruin the dog's front and shoulders permanently for the show-ring.

All dogs should be taught 'no', and that this means 'no'. To stop a dog pulling on the lead a folded newspaper or light branch is required and, as the dog pulls forward into its collar, a tap is delivered on the nose with the command 'no'. If this is repeated everytime the dog pulls it will soon stop.

Depending on the purpose for which the dog is required, it may be useful to teach it to sit on command. This I do not recommend for a showdog as they must stand in the ring.

Personally I teach my dogs very little, but they all walk on the lead without pulling, know 'no', with particular reference to livestock and poultry, the command 'go in', and to come when called. They are also taught to be left tied up either to a post, if working, or to a bench or radiator pipe for showing, without screaming their heads off. These seem to be the basic requirements for my life with Borders as workers, showdogs and friends.

No maintenance book is handed out with a new dog as much of the caring for a dog comes from instinct.

A good warm, draughtproof bed is a prime requirement, be it in the house or kennel. In the house this should be tucked away in a quiet place to which the dog can retreat to his 'den' should he want to rest. All dogs need to sleep for long periods throughout the day.

My own dogs are kennelled in individual kennels so that every dog has its own sleeping house, with a box inside, and run. In the run I have a wooden table with legs sawn off to provide a low bench for the dog to sit on, off the concrete: this they really appreciate. As my kennels are all in a row, the dogs have the companionship of their neighbours. I prefer to keep them separate, ever since a fight between two bitches who lived together happily for years, until I was careless about reintroducing them after one had been away to be mated. Since then I have decided to avoid fights at all costs.

Should a fight start there are several basic rules to remember. Keep calm yourself, remove any dogs who have not joined in and shut them securely and safely away. Never try to pull the opponents apart—this causes worse injuries—but push them TOGETHER until you can separate them. It is extremely difficult to separate two fighting Borders as their method of fighting is to lock onto each other. It may be possible to separate them should they shift their grip, in that fleeting second. Otherwise one has to resort to various tricks. Shaking the pepper-pot over them, twisting ears, burning noses with cigarettes, dousing them in a water-trough or the bath full of water may all work but, even then, the combatants will leave go only for a moment and then you should quickly pick one up and keep it high out of reach. Throw it into a pen, over the garden-gate, anywhere long enough to put one of them away. If all else fails, the old "terrier-man's" trick of simultaneously inserting a sharpened pencil up the rectum of each dog usually works. Do be careful not to be bitten yourself, once the dogs have left go for that second, as they will grab out again at each other the moment they realise they have been separated.

Borders as a rule are not fighters, and will live together in packs for years, but once they do start, they are the very devil to part, and will never forget. Therefore my advice is not to take risks. Three dogs or bitches in any breed should never be kennelled together as, should a quarrel arise, two will gang up together and do untold damage to the third.

My preference for material for kennels is a wooden house, a concrete run, with fine weld-mesh netting buried in the concrete for three inches. This netting is rather pricey but it has several advantages to make it worth the extra expense, if possible. The dogs cannot chew the wire, so cannot damage and loosen their teeth. They cannot climb up it as the mesh is too close to get a toehold. They cannot push their noses through and rub off their whiskers. All of which are favourite Border pastimes!

Exercise is required but maybe not as much as some breeds. Borders will thrive just as well with a trip to the post box and a run in the garden as with a two or three mile hike every day. The quality of the exercise is more important than the duration. A short stretch of controlled road walking on a lead, not pulling as this puts muscle on the shoulders, followed by a good free gallop is the best exercise. Should the hindquarters need development, walking over rough ground will help considerably: really rough tussocky grass or thick heather being ideal. This makes the dog use the stifle and hock when picking its feet up. Walking up a hill, without pulling, will have the same effect. I know one young lady who spent hours 'improving' her Labrador by walking her up a bridge over a railway, this being the only incline in an otherwise flat piece of country—where there's a will there's a way.

Small puppies require short periods of play followed by sleep, as do adolescents. A growing animal should never be worn out to the limit of its efforts.

The inoculations have been dealt with elsewhere, as has the need for worming. If there is evidence of the presence of tapeworm (segments in the droppings, staring coat, emaciated thinness, ravenous appetite, smelling breath) these should be dealt with by a dose obtained from the Veterinary Surgeon.

Borders thrive on very little food so their figures should be watched at all times. My own dogs have one main meal per day, in the evening, and a snack breakfast, in the winter only, which consists of a Bonio biscuit or a couple of ginger biscuits. Should one require fattening up I give it rice pudding for breakfast as a supplement to the main meal. The main meal consists of two-thirds soaked terrier meal with one-third of whatever meat is available. Occasionally I feed fish instead of meat. A word of warning about feeding Borders: they have been known to choke to death whilst feeding, so all meat should be chopped up fine and biscuitmeal well soaked. There are people who will scoff at this advice. Two of my own Borders have died in this way, not on lumps of meat but just eating their soaked meal, and I can assure the reader that it is worth the extra trouble in going through the food for lumps if this can prevent such a distressing occurrence. Vegetables are cooked for my dogs: spinach, carrots, cabbage, onions (very good worm preventers) and nettles in summer, all go into the saucepan with the meat or fish. Personally, I do not use the 'complete diets' for dogs: although convenient and the lazy man's way of feeding, I prefer to know as far as possible what my dogs are eating and to vary the content as I think fit from day to day and dog to dog. When feeding nettles care should be taken to avoid any that may have been sprayed with weed-killer for obvious reasons.

Once a week my dogs receive a flat beef rib-bone to chew. This they thoroughly enjoy. It helps to keep their teeth clean and also gives them something to do. As soon as these bones are chewed down to a short stump they must be removed as this can become wedged across the top of the mouth and is extremely difficult to dislodge. Game bones and chicken or turkey bones must be avoided as these can splinter and perforate the innards of the dog. Heavy knuckle bones are not advisable for Borders, as the sheer weight of these on the lower jaws as the dog carries them around could cause the teeth to be pulled out of line. The round sections of bone filled with marrow, although delectable, again are not recommended for show Borders, as the nose pushed against the inside of the bone while the dog licks out the marrow will cause the whiskers on the face to be scraped off.

It is important to handle a Border regularly to feel what the condition is underneath the coat. Appearances can be very deceptive especially as the coat thickens. Borders become fat very easily; they also run off weight very quickly too. When the old coat is dying-off the Border may become very thin, which does not show except by handling the dog. It seems that changing a coat takes a tremendous lot out of the dog, and it will not put weight back, without extra food, until the new coat is growing well.

Water should be accessible but should not be left down overnight where rodents might pass as, should they urinate into it, the dogs who drink from it may well become infected with various unpleasant and sometimes lethal diseases.

The anal gland (under the tail) may require squeezing

from time to time. This varies from dog to dog, but some Borders are very prone to trouble here. There is a nack to this job, which may be learnt from an experienced breeder or a Veterinary Surgeon. Should it not be possible to learn this, a Veterinary Surgeon will attend to this for the owner. Signs that this needs attention are the dog 'tobogganing' on its behind, biting around the root of the tail, unpleasant breath, or breaking out in patches of eczema around the hindquarters.

Every dog owner should have in his first aid kit an animal thermometer. The temperature is taken by inserting the bulb of this into the rectum, taking care the dog does not sit down during the performance. The normal temperature of an adult is 102°, a puppy may be a fraction more.

Other items needed are flea powder, an eye-wash solution and good eye ointment, canker powder for ears, and an anti-biotic powder or ointment should the dog be working. Friars balsam I find useful for pink sores between the pads (caused I think by fungii picked up off damp leaves). There is a marvellous remedy for growing hair back onto patches, by the name of Bob Grasses Skincure: this is a rather messy but invaluable preparation.

Should the dog look ill, of course the advice of the Veterinary Surgeon should be sought immediately.

In my experience, Borders have the most remarkable healing ability. The most gruesome tears heal up in a matter of days. In this respect they live up to their tough reputation. But, on the other hand, I never have a general anæsthetic for a Border unless absolutely necessary, as they can and do pass out under this. There seems to be something in their makeup which just stops for no apparent reason.

The tough, unspoiled, reputation does not mean that the Border does not require looking after just as much as any other dog.

The normal Border is a healthy dog. A fine instance of this was the late Dandyhow Brussel Sprout. At the time of his death, aged sixteen, this dog had all his teeth, admittedly worn down a little, but all present. On checking his record at the surgery it was found that this dog had visited it but once, for a booster innoculation. He certainly had not run up any large bills for his owners!

In my experience I have found that the Border lives to a ripe old age, if it can weather a dangerous age that there seems to be for them between the ages of five and eight. This I cannot account for but have noticed many Borders do die at that age and once over that they go on and on, for anything between thirteen to sixteen years.

Once life has become a burden to an elderly dog, it should kindly be helped over the last hurdle. To keep an old dog who is suffering either physically, or mentally if it cannot go out with the others on hunting days, is entirely selfish and no kindness. It is an awful decision to have to make, to part with a dearly loved friend, but this is one of the responsibilities of owning a dog, and should not be shirked.

As I may have sounded rather gloomy in parts of this chapter, I should like to say that one should positively enjoy the companionship of one's dogs, as they enjoy ours. The normal dog will have a happy and comparatively trouble-free life, and these are the times one remembers in the years to come, so one should live and enjoy every minute one can with such versatile companions and loyal friends.

CHAPTER 8

Showing and Hunt Terrier Shows

Having made a careful choice of a puppy the owner will no doubt start to think of showing it, as it approaches the age of six months.

To a beginner this may seem such a terrifying prospect that they will be put off before they actually start through sheer apprehension. For the removal of this terror I will try to explain the procedure at both Kennel Club and Hunt Terrier Shows.

I will deal with the Kennel Club Shows first. To be exhibited at any show, except an Exemption Show, a dog must be registered with the Kennel Club, and also any transfer of ownership must be recorded at the Kennel Club. The completed registration form, or transfer form, must be obtained at the time of the purchase of the dog from the person from whom the dog is purchased. These are then forwarded together with the appropriate fee to the Kennel Club and in due course a certificate of registration or transfer will be received from them.

Before embarking on a show it is advisable to find out whether there are either ringcraft classes or match meetings held by any local canine society. Here, for a modest fee, both dog and owner can learn basic ringcraft, and so have conquered any stage fright before spending a larger sum entering a show. Besides being invaluable to dog and owner, these evenings are an enjoyable social event in a relaxed and friendly atmosphere with everyone having lots of time to chat and help the newcomer.

There are five categories of show: Exemption, which are chiefly held in the summer months and run in conjunction with the local féte or village show; Sanction, which cater for puppies and novice exhibits chiefly; Limited, which includes all dogs except those which have won a Challenge Certificate; Open at which Champions and Challenge Certificate winners may compete; and Championship, which are rather serious affairs and more expensive to enter.

The beginner should not be too ambitious in the choice of his first show. One of the smaller local shows, or an open show, should be selected and only one or two classes entered for the first venture. The most important factor at a dog's first show is that it should enjoy itself — whatever happens awardwise is of little significance as, provided the exhibit has no unhappy associations with this first venture, it will have plenty of time later to win prizes, provided it is good enough of course.

The preparation of the Border is dealt with in a later chapter, but if possible it should be presented in an eight to twelve weeks growth of new coat all over, to look its best, and in muscular condition, but not too thin or too fat.

Entries must be sent in advance so the entry form must have been carefully completed, signed and sent off with the correct fees by the date which is printed on the schedule for entries closing. It is a good idea to form a habit of writing the name of the dog and classes entered on the front of the schedule and, when one is in the full swing of the show season, to have two files, one for schedules with entries closing and the other of the shows for which entries have been sent. Should the registration or transfer of the dog be in the hands of the Kennel Club, the initials N.A.F. (name applied for) and T.A.F. (transfer applied for) must follow the name of the dog on the entry form. Some Exemption shows will accept entries at the show.

The following items will be needed at the show: collar and lead, a finer show lead, brush, comb, small dish for drinking water, at a 'benched' show a chain is compulsory and a blanket or towel for the dog to lie upon is also needed, a small cellophane bag containing some of the dog's favourite titbits (liver, chicken, yeast tablets or ginger biscuits all being favourites), a safety pin for the ring number, and any exhibitor's passes which may have been sent, not forgetting the schedule and appropriate dog!

If possible, it is advisable to arrive in plenty of time as then one can find a quiet corner in which to sit and allow the dog to have time to accustom itself to the new surroundings. It may be possible to have a practice walk up and down the ring with the dog before the show starts, which is helpful to puppies but not generally necessary for experienced dogs unless they have developed some quirk in their showmanship.

The ring number will either be collected from the secretary's table or handed out by the stewards in the ring. Sometimes they are sent through the post.

Different judges make very slight variations in judging so it is worth watching carefully. Should the newcomer be in the first class he should try to arrange to be amongst the last dogs to be seen by the judge so that he has plenty of time to see the procedure, and for both himself and the dog to settle down.

A dog that is barking or misbehaving should be avoided with a puppy, as this can frighten them. Never be afraid to move your position in the ring (unless of course placed there by the judge) if the dog next door is having an adverse effect on your dog. As one becomes more experienced one selects intelligently where one stands. I try to stand next to certain people whose dogs I know never misbehave. If I am showing an immature bitch puppy I try not to stand next to a well grown and developed dog puppy, which will make mine look even more immature.

Usual procedure is for the judge to ask to see all the dogs moving around the ring together, a couple of times. The dog should be on the inside of the ring where the judge can see it without having to peer past trousers and skirts of the handler. This is the time when the basic training of walking on a lead without pulling comes into service. The pace that the judge wishes to see is that of the dog stepping out at a brisk walk.

In turn the dogs are examined on the table by the judge. There are some judges who prefer to judge them on the ground but they are in the minority. The judge may ask the age of the dog so this information should be ready on the tongue tip. As the dog next to yours walks up and down the ring, put your dog on the table, standing him in his best posture held with a hand under the head and tail-tip, the handler being the far side of the dog from the judge. This should have been practiced at home and the dog should be prepared to be handled all over, including teeth (jaws shut) and to be spanned behind the shoulders with two hands. The dog and handler will then be required to walk at a brisk walk once or twice up and down the ring—or they may be asked to move in a triangle—away from the judge to one corner of the ring, across the end, and back to the judge on the diagonal. The dog must always be on the same side as the judge, when viewed from the side.

Many beginners suffer the most awful 'butterflies' before showing their dog. I offer the following cold comfort— all eyes are upon the dog not the exhibitor, who could well appear stark naked and go unnoticed!

Having examined every dog in turn, the judge will make his selection which are then placed in order of merit in the centre of the ring and prize cards are awarded. The money may or may not be attached to the card. Should there be a voucher attached this should be removed at once and put carefully away until cashed at the prize money payout office.

A dog which is lucky enough to win first prize in all its classes is known as an unbeaten dog and may be required to compete for the best of breed or best in show awards.

Many people are disheartened if their dog does not win awards at once. It is well worth persevering, as Borders vary tremendously from day to day with coat and condition. Should the dog consistently not gain any recognition it would be advisable to ask several of the top breeders whether there is any fault which is preventing this. If it has a really bad fault it is better to save the entry money and try again with another dog.

Sooner or later, every novice who has had a considerable run of success, which will probably diminish as their exhibit progresses by virtue of its wins into higher classes and therefore stronger competition, or whose second exhibit may not achieve such success as their first one did, will declare that it is all a twist anyway and that only faces are judged. Anyone who has this feeling, be they the beginner or the seasoned exhibitor, would do well to stop and consider their dogs. The trouble always stems from the dog. If it is good enough, and fit enough, it will win as far as it deserves to, on merit. If it is not good enough it wont, no matter who is on the other end of the lead. Kennel blindness, i.e. the inability to see the faults in one's own dogs, is a deadly disease to the exhibitor and will put him out of the show-ring quicker than any run of real bad luck. To stick at the game one must be able to see the faults and virtues in one's own stock. The art of clever breeding is to improve upon the faults without losing the benefit of the virtues: this can never be achieved unless one realises the faults are there. So if you feel that the dice is loaded against you consider your dog against its peers, and next time, either by breeding or selection, try to improve upon this dog. If the fault is merely one of conditioning or presentation this can soon be rectified. The well known breeders will give helpful advice on how to improve the animal in this respect.

The art of handling a Border in the show-ring can only be mastered with practice. By the very nature of the breed they tend to be rather heavy in hand in the show-ring, not being gassy and assertive characters towards other dogs as a general rule.

There are one or two excellent handlers of Borders. Mr. Robert Hall and Mr. Ted Hutchinson both having a magic touch as far as showing the breed is concerned.

Often a puppy will start its career showing very gaily on a loose lead only to become rather bored after a few shows, whereupon the tail will hang down instead of wagging. A true specialist judge will appreciate that this is merely the breed character coming to the fore and will not penalise the dog merely for not wagging its tail. All-round judges tend to prefer a happier aura and of course the wagging tail, well carried, is eye-catching.

The ideal way to show a Border is on a loose lead but rather than have a dog standing in a position resembling a rain-soaked donkey it is better to 'set them up'. The judge wants to see the best in the dog and it is up to the handler to present the dog to best advantage.

It is important to learn the correct position to set-up a dog. The number of experienced exhibitors who set-up their Borders, on the table for the judge to see, in the most ghastly positions never ceases to amaze me.

I was fortunate very early in my showing career to be taken on one side by an old-time Scottie exhibitor, who was no doubt appalled by my bungling handling efforts, who spent some considerable time teaching me how to stand a dog in the correct position and why. Although this kind person has been dead for many years now I frequently remember him with gratitude for the time and consideration he gave to a raw novice.

Often one sees a Border plonked on the judge's table with forelegs sticking out in front of the dog and the hindquarters placed under the dog and closer together than the front legs with the weight of the dog suspended by its tail which is held in a vice-like grip from the exhibitor's hand.

The dog should be correctly balanced. By that I mean balance as used in connection with the horse, i.e. standing on all four feet with the weight of the dog taken back on its hocks. An imaginary plumb-line dropped from the withers to the ground should fall behind the foreleg. In too many Borders this line would actually fall in front of the foreleg on account of a straight shoulder, giving a very unbalanced animal.

To set-up the dog the forelegs should be placed under the dog, not too narrow and not wide-apart. The feet should all point forwards. The hindquarters should be placed (NOT by the tail) slightly behind the dog, in a comfortable position. If placed too far out the dog will not be able to stand on them. They should take the weight of the dog, the stifles should be bent and the hindleg below the hock should be perpendicular to the ground. The hindquarters must be wider apart than the front legs, and the hocks must turn neither in nor out. The tail is supported by resting it on the hand and the angle of this should be practiced to achieve the best result for the dog. For example, if you are showing a dog with very straight stifles and poor angulation in the hocks do not hold the tail in such a position that it is a continuation of the straight line of the hindleg. The head and neck should be carried higher than the point of the withers. One sometimes sees Borders presented with the head as the lowest point in the topline. Nor should the head be raised so that the dog is stargazing, i.e. pointing its nose to heaven. The ideal is a slightly crested neck with the head pointing slightly down from it—see the photographs of Ch. True Temper and Ch. Portholme Magic.

125

It is important for both the handler and the dog to practice standing the dog in the correct position on the table. I start my puppies at about six weeks so that they grow into the habit of adopting the correct stance, with the weight correctly distributed.

Some people tend to panic when handling their Borders in the show-ring and, without looking to see whether the dog is standing right or not, adopt a nervous habit of yanking the wretched animal's backend up by its tail and dropping the hindquarters into a new position. Look and see if the dog is standing correctly and, if it is, leave well alone.

Another mistake that is made is to feel that the people kneeling down to set-up their dogs have an advantage over the free-showing dog. I have seen people throw away their advantage by seizing a perfectly good showman and setting him up just because those on either side were setting theirs up. Dogs that show on a loose lead look so much nicer than those topped and tailed, especially if the latter is done badly.

Should your dog have a fault do not fiddle with that part of the dog. Leave it alone and aim its good points at the judge. Fiddling with ears, elbows, stifles or tails only serves to draw everyone's attention to the fault—particularly if this is done at show after show. If your dog has rotten quarters but a good head and front show it so that the judge sees the front end rather than the back, and vice versa should the quarters be better than the front.

Mr. Hall, I know, practices showing his dogs on his lawn and wall-top for many hours and thus presents his exhibits in the best possible position for each dog, well schooled and moving at the right pace to suit the dog. It was a joy to watch the rapport between himself and Ch. Deerstone Destiny who he showed on a loose lead, moving him around and letting him stand in good attitudes at the end of the lead.

Mr. Ted Hutchinson has an extraordinary knack of making any Border show. His own exhibits are always well schooled but he demonstrated his skill recently by taking over a bitch which did not know him, but which was known to be an extremely dour shower, always making the worst of herself. Within ten minutes Ted had her showing like a dream, wagging her tail and carrying herself with pride. It was an amazing transformation and one which I relished witnessing.

The local Border Terrier Club will probably hold three shows a year, which may be a Limited, Open and Championship show. There may also be Match Meetings, and other enjoyable social events.

A Kennel Club Challenge Certificate ('C.C.') is on offer to the best exhibit of each sex at a Championship show. This highly sought after award is by no means an automatic award as the judges are specifically instructed to "refrain from awarding Challenge Certificates unless the winning exhibit in each sex is of such outstanding merit as to be worthy of the title of Champion". Therefore for any dog to be awarded such an accolade is no mean achievement. Three such awards under three different judges qualify the dog for the title of champion — the ambition of us all! Should the animal win three or more Challenge Certificates whilst under the age of twelve months, it must win a further Challenge Certificate over the age of twelve months before it can become a champion.

My favourite shows are Open shows for all breeds where a few classes for Borders are scheduled — particularly if held in conjunction with an Agricultural show. These I thoroughly enjoy, as do I showing my Borders in variety classes at any shows. I regret to say that Championship shows I enjoy less and less; they tend to be rather too important, and the days too long, very often involving a seventeen or eighteen hour marathon.

The hunt terrier shows are a very different kettle of fish! As there is no governing body over these shows, there are no hard and fast regulations.

The shows are advertised in the local newspapers, and maybe Horse and Hound and the Shooting Times.

No registrations are necessary, in fact pet names are the order of the day, 'Peg' being preferable to 'Peg of My Heart' on such occasions. The entries are handed in on arrival, usually either into a tent or a horse-trailer which is serving as secretary's office for the day.

The judging procedure varies so much that it is impossible to generalise upon the form it will take. The dogs may be asked to walk round the ring; if so one will immediately notice that the pace is funereal compared to the brisk 'Kennel Club' walk. The terrier may be examined standing on a board laid on the ground—the examination being anything from a fairly thorough going-over to a long stare and a look at the teeth. The dog may or may not be seen moving.

After some lengthy discussion—there are usually two judges—the winners may or may not be placed in order in the ring. Sometimes the results are decided by the losers leaving the ring as discarded and the numbers of the winners being written down and handed to the secretary, who then announces them over the loudspeaker, after they have all left the ring. On other occasions the winners are placed in a more orthodox, and to my mind clearer and more courteous manner, thus enabling everyone to understand what is happening. There will be a championship class for all the class winners.

These shows are judged by huntsmen and Masters of Hounds and sometimes, as a great honour, by someone who is considered to know a good working terrier. The dogs are not judged to the Kennel Club Standard, but to the general 'likeliness' for work. Surely there must be cause for reflection here as, although a great many of our top Champions can and do compete and win at these shows, I fear that many others would not be given a second glance. On the other hand I usually come away from a hunt terrier show whether as a spectator or competitor, win or lose, with a feeling of frustration that the good dogs very often do not get justice. Very recently I watched a Border and Lakeland class being judged, where the winner was undeniably a very nice terrier, Lakeland, but the others which followed were abysmal looking types which no one in their senses would want as a working terrier—all with varying degrees of Lakeland ancestry. The poor Borders, very reasonable specimens too, were all given the boot. We afterwards learnt the so-called terrier expert/huntsman judge "could not abide they Borders". I felt it would have served him right had he really had to use those other miserable little specimens for work in his profession.

However, there must be something about these shows which grips people as they have a large following of regular showgoers who show every weekend during the summer months at such events.

To me, the highlight of these shows is the terrier-racing. This takes place when the serious judging has been completed and is usually run in heats.

A fox's brush attached to a very long string is connected to a bicycle-wheel at the other end of the field. The brush usually, for the sake of avoiding fights, ends up by conveniently going to ground under some haybales.

The terriers are lined-up, about six at a time, or, in more sophisticated areas, are put into starting traps. The fox's brush is then waved under each dog's nose to arouse the competitive spirit—though by this time the shindy of barking terriers is so great that nothing needs arousing! The cycle wheel starts turning, and they're off! All hell is let loose—very often bystanding terriers slip their leads and join the race—more often than not it all ends in a furious mêlée of fighting terriers half way up the track—in which case they are all separated and back they all go to square one. These little dogs really do burn up the ground and the poor old cyclist has to go flat out with hands or feet at the other end to prevent these keen tykes from catching the brush in mid-field. The heats are patiently re-run until a satisfactory conclusion has been reached. As far as I can surmise, the only rule is 'three bites and the dog is disqualified'—and you can't say fairer than that. I believe that terriers really enjoy this racing and one can spot the experts from the alacrity with which they start. However, I would not recommend this as a Sunday afternoon sport for a budding Champion as canine tempers do become short sometimes and fights are not uncommon, and I certainly would not recommend anyone to take a known fighter for terrier-racing, the temptations would be irresistible!

To anyone who has never witnessed this wonderful comedy show, I say, do go along—it is the greatest fun— whether they are racing as if at the White City, or "mixing it"! For family entertainment this is worth a guinea a minute.

CHAPTER 9

Coat Preparation and Colour

Claims are often made that the Border Terrier is a non-trim breed. This might be true in that one does not need a pair of clippers to prepare one for show, but on the other hand it is very misleading to sell someone a Border puppy and allow them to believe that they need never touch its coat. Although they do moult hair most of the time, Borders never cast their coat right out as does a Labrador, except a bitch after breeding a litter.

Most Borders will require stripping twice a year. This entails removing completely the heavy overcoat which will grow very shaggy and unkempt looking if left. Many pet Borders which are not stripped will grow layer upon layer of coat and will be seen to resemble the coconut doormat more and more as time progresses.

It is not at all difficult to strip a Border. The only equipment needed is either your finger and thumb, or a BLUNT penknife or a stripping knife with a serrated edge which can be bought at most big shows.

As the top coat grows it will reach the stage where the dog looks distinctly shaggy with the hair on the back falling into a natural parting. This is the indication that the dog should be stripped. To test whether the coat is ready to take off, pull a small tuft from the back by a sharp tug in the direction in which the hair grows. If this comes out easily, the dog is ready to strip. If the hair does not come off without resistance it should be left for another week or so, and then tested again.

For convenience most people stand their dogs on a table to strip, as this saves backache and the dog is also easier to manage. However one can strip anywhere, and one young lady (who actually has a diploma for stripping, which has caused her young men considerable anxiety when first they have heard of it!) sits on the floor holding the dog with her knees rather as if she were sheep-shearing.

Using either your first finger and thumb, or the thumb against the edge of the penknife blade or trimming knife, pull the hair, a little at a time, with short sharp tugs, in the direction in which it grows. Provided that the coat is ready to come off, and it is pulled quickly, the dog will not mind, once it realises that you are not going to hurt—in fact they seem to appreciate the tidy feeling after they have been stripped.

I start with the back and work a strip towards the tail. The tail can be done gradually by taking a little off above and below, at this stage, for about an inch or two up the tail from the root. This grows in quite quickly, and one can do another inch in a week or so, thus keeping the short thick shape without reducing the whole thing to a rat's tail which takes months to grow back to shape.

It is very useful to teach the dog to lie out flat when doing the sides. If it struggles and cannot be held down single-handed it is helpful to remember that a dog whose head is pinned to the ground cannot gain the necessary leverage to get up, and, by enlisting help to hold the head down, one can wield the trimming knife in one hand and use the other to hold the body of the dog flat. I find that most dogs will soon give in and lie perfectly still.

Having done the back, sides and as far as possible, without pulling the softer hairs, under the tummy, I then return to the neck and front, paying particular attention to the direction of growth of the hair here, as there are many seams and swirls around this area.

On the head I remove all hair on the skull, except for a few eyebrow hairs left to give expression. In front of

132

the eyes any whiskers which are sticking up and which might irritate the eyes or interfere with the vision of the dog are pulled out, as are any hairs above or on the side of the eyes which may enter the eye. This point I watch at all times, as it must be uncomfortable for the dog to have hairs growing or falling into the eyes, and can even cause the eye to ulcerate in bad cases. Taking care to preserve the moustache or whisker, I remove any very long hairs in the beard, and all hair on the cheekbones. The dead hair on the ears is removed gently by hand, and any tufts inside the ears, again for the comfort of the dog.

The forelegs are then smoothed off down the front, any dead hair being removed and the knees flattened off. There is a fringe growing up the back of the front legs which I even-off by hand, removing the points on the elbows. The feet are generally trimmed with scissors. There is an art in doing this to look natural which only comes with practice.

We are now left with the underparts and rear of the dog. This is when help may have to be enlisted, particularly with a youngster. The brisket and tummy are done with the dog lying on its back, or standing up on its hindlegs supported against a wall with a hand for steadiness. The hair on the ribcage and brisket is pulled as for the sides, but when the softer hairs on the tummy and inside the thighs are reached it is more humane to snip these off as it really does hurt the dog to have these pulled. A male will look smarter, besides being more hygienic, if the long hairs are snipped off the end of the sheath of the penis carefully. To do the trousers either have someone to hold the head of the dog and to prevent it from sitting down, or, should no helper be around, a lead tied to a hook above the table is just as effective. These parts are done with finger and thumb, or stripping knife, as for the main parts of the dog.

The coat should be taken right down so that the soft undercoat of the dog is left and there are no bristles stick-

133

ing up through it. Should the weather be chilly or damp, it is kinder to remove the coat a little at a time so that the dog will not feel the sudden change in temperature too much.

After about three weeks, use the serrated edge of the stripping knife, or the penknife blade, to scrape along the back and sides of the dog and down the outside of the thighs, to remove some of the undercoat which will by now be lifting slightly. This enables the new coat to grow more evenly.

Should odd hairs of topcoat remain, a sandpaper block used as a brush will soon remove them.

If the dog is a companion or pet it should not need any more attention to the coat, apart from brushing and combing and removal of tufts from the eyes and under the tail, until it begins to look shaggy again in six months' time.

Individual coats vary enormously. There are those, which literally do not need stripping, which just need the odd hair picking off from time to time. These dogs have an excellent topcoat with harsh and thick individual hairs, and an undercoat of a lighter colour.

Some Borders do have soft coats which are extremely difficult to present for show, and not what is required for work. These dogs appear rather woolly most of the time, and are generally rather a washy colour, with a light coloured and silky topknot which is probably inherited from the early origins of the breed with Bedlington and Dandie Dinmont Terriers.

Another coat which one meets, and which does not require stripping, is a short, hard single coat, this gives the dog a very neat appearance but is totally unacceptables either for show or on a working dog as it offers no protection against weather, and consequently is dead against the Standard. However, on a household pet, this might prove an asset requiring no attention and remaining neat looking at all times, although such a coat is not a desirable breed characteristic and untypical of the breed.

The owners of 'trimmed' terriers appear to think that all we do to prepare a Border for show is to catch it, find a piece of binder-twine, and off we go. This may have been the practice in byegone times by certain well-known personalities, but nowadays a great deal of care and preparation is taken before a show.

The effect required is of a workmanlike yet shapely dog, with a rough tweed finish. Mr. Ted Hutchinson and Mr. Bob Williams are both masters of this art and I study their dogs for hours to see which hairs are removed and which are left. To present a Border without it appearing presented is the skill.

Ideally, a Border is always in coat, but in practice most Borders are in coat some eight to twelve weeks after stripping, and then perhaps with constant attention one can keep the coat going for another month or so—this means that they are virtually in coat for sixteen weeks out of fifty-two, which I think one of the biggest drawbacks to the breed as a serious showdog. One can know that a judge loves one's dog, and yet never manage to have it in coat when that judge is on the woolsack.

With a certain amount of experience one might be able to aim one's dog at certain shows, but the growth of the coat depends very much on the individual dog, and also on the weather conditions and the season of the year. Of course, if one is lucky enough to have one of the true non-strip coats this is no problem, but in my experience I never breed these on my best show dogs.

When stripping for show, never allow the neck to start growing a new coat before the back, otherwise you will end up with a show dog with a ruff in front and a tapering body. Also, should any mishap befall such as your Border burning a hole or chewing a patch, or your attempts at tidying-up making a hole, the only remedy is to strip the dog right down and start again, otherwise the patch will never match the rest of the dog again!

135

When a bitch is in good coat she comes into season, no doubt nature's way of making sure she is at her most beautiful to the dog, but not entirely helpful to the owner trying to campaign her for top awards. Many people do not show bitches in season. Personally I do, if I want to, taking care not to upset any dogs. I know the majority of exhibitors do show them, but it is significant to note that when discussing this with a group of exhibitors recently, we all agreed that we had never had any outstanding wins with a bitch in season—presumably as they are feeling a little 'off' at the time. To confound the theory, I do know of one extremely perverse terrier, not a Border, who only won top honours when in season!

Brood bitches after puppies will throw all their coat, including the tail and most of the face furnishing. As a bitch is in her best coat when in season, by the time she is due to whelp her coat has blown. It is a help at whelping time to clean out all the long hair around the hindquarters, and around the nipples, so that the puppies can find them with ease and are not inhaling hair. Some people strip their bitch at this time. I have done it with no ill-effect, although I was told that the litter would be born hairless—unfortunately there was no litter in that instance, so I never proved or disproved the truth of this, what I suspect must be an old wives' tale! However, I doubt if one gains much by stripping out at this time, as although the coat of the bitch will be ready for show some eight weeks after her whelping, and, provided that the puppies are weaned early, her figure will be respectable, she will not have regained her muscletone and will not be moving her best.

The coat of a Border should never be trimmed—that is cut or clipped. The possible exception to this rule being around feet, the belly-hair and on the inside of the thighs, but I know that purists would never agree to this. The texture of the coat will be ruined by persistent cutting. If the coat is clipped tight waves will appear in the new coat. Besides which the general rough-edged effect is lost through the straight edges left by scissors or clipper marks. It has become the fashion to cut around the tail with scissors, a very lazy habit which I deplore and which I hope will soon become unfashionable. This ruins the look of an otherwise carefully presented dog.

Undercoat should be left in; this no doubt sounds a direct contradiction to my earlier advice to comb it out when the new coat is growing through. Once there are no longer any ridges of undercoat sticking up, leave well alone.

Borders who are regularly worked do not need stripping. They require every bit of rugged coat and undercoat for their work. This protects them against weather, wet drains, sitting around for hours in icy conditions whilst other terriers are working, against thorns and spikes and against bites and injury from their quarry. When crawling and squeezing through tight spots they strip off any loose hairs against the edges. They have been known to emerge beautifully stripped having gone to ground looking like the hearthrug. Working Borders will lose the furnishing on their face and around the eyes.

A judge of calibre should be able to spot a good dog whatever the presentation, which is a very temporary thing. Should the basic DOG be right, and the coat textures correct, the dog should not be penalised for a rough appearance or loss of face furnishing. Judges must remember that a Border is first and foremost a working terrier—they are not meant to be pretty but a utility terrier.

Hedges, fences, rose-bushes, heather, rockery and gravel are all used by Borders who are not hand-stripped but who obviously feel much better with some of the dead hair removed. One well-known stud dog in the Windermere area kept himself very smart with the aid of a box hedge around the rose-borders.

A young puppy of around ten weeks will develop a fuzz, which is the original puppy coat. This is very easily removed with finger and thumb.

137

Puppies who are not thriving, or adults who have had a virus or a set-back very often grow a light coloured coat which stands-off from the dog. This is known as poverty coat, and, once the animal tones up and the follicles receive correct nourishment, the new coat will grow as usual and the poverty coat should be stripped off.

Some Borders have a rather greasy coat. I have found an excellent remedy for this is either to wash the dog in a medicated-type shampoo, or to bathe the skin with a solution of three-quarters surgical spirit shaken up with quarter Dettol. Never wash a Border just before a show.

A soft coated Border's coat can be improved by perpetual stripping, although the texture will never be as good as that of a correctly coated dog.

Coat texture varies slightly depending on the growth of the coat. It could generally be said to harden as the coat grows, and then as the coat starts to blow and die, the texture becomes softer again.

Now to coat colour, about which very little seems known. The colours mentioned in the Standard are red, wheaten, grizzle and tan and blue and tan, although one will find a variety of colours given on registration certificates. The reason for this is that it is not easy to tell accurately the colour of a very young puppy—several dark grizzles go through life registered as blue and tan and reds as grizzle. Generally speaking the colour of the adult will be lighter than the colour of the same dog as a puppy.

Borders come in the agouti (grey-brindled) range of colour, as does the Dandie Dinmont. Wheaten comes from the same source as the liver Bedlington, and used to carry liver noses and light coloured pads. It is thought that the show people bred out these tendencies, and at the same time the gene for modifying (dilution) of the black, which is why one does not see the true blue Borders. These were known as saddleblacks and were distinct from the blue and tan which we see today. Saddlebacks, as their name depicts, carried a definite saddle which was a silver-blue in colour, often with a very light strip down the spine, and the rest of the dog including the neck was wheaten. The undercoat was also wheaten. The blue and tan which is seen nowadays is a much darker colour, generally with a redder tan, and the dark colour runs from the neck to the tail and right down the ribs of the dog; the undercoat is blue.

The true wheaten is rarely seen today. This is a light straw colour and the muzzle and ears are generally a dusky blue. Wheaten is a distinct colour, not a washy indeterminate light red. It is a clear colour with no grizzling, just the blue ears and muzzle and a blue ring on the tail where the blues and grizzles have a lighter ring, about a third of the length of the tail from the root. This is identical to the colour of the Soft Coated Wheaten Terrier.

Miss Garnett Orme, from whom I gleamed the above information, and others told me that blue and tans mated together will breed darker and darker backs on each generation. She told me that the best blue and tan colour would be bred by mating a blue and tan to a wheaten as these colours are genetically connected. The inheritance of the blue and tan is not a simple recessive, as breeders who have tried to breed this colour have found when they received perpetual surprises in the colours of their litters. I was very surprised to breed three in a litter of four puppies from two grizzle parents. On that occasion it had never entered my head that I should breed any, although on other occasions I have expected some and not bred any.

The line of definition between a real blue grizzle and a blue and tan is very vague. There are some dogs registered as blue grizzles who were definitely blue and tan, and some which I just do not know to this day which colour they were. The dark black and tans are very unattractive and not a typical Border colour as the black is very black and the tan a hot tan more reminiscent of a Welsh than a Border Terrier.

Red varies from a very bright copper colour through to a washy sandy shade, the former usually carries a very black mask and ears when young. The black mask fades as the Border matures, and by the time it has turned two will usually be a dark grey, and will finish up white. Very richly coloured red Borders often turn very white in their faces, along their backs and feet at about five years old. Many of the Portholme dogs did this, they were a very good red in colour when young.

There are always a handful of blue and tans in the ring, but there remains a strong colour prejudice against them, both from judges and the general public, who will reject perfectly good puppies saying "that is not a Border Terrier colour". It is difficult to win top honours with a blue. The reason for this being, I think, that judges do not realise that the colour is broken up around the shoulders, and thus the dog appears to dip in back whereas actually it does not.

Grizzle and tan describes the 'heather-mixture' colour of the breed. The individual hairs are light at the base, red in the middle, and black tipped, and when laid against each other present a most pleasing effect of light mixed with dark, with red tinges. The depth of colour varies with the individual, Ch. Dandyhow Shady Knight and his daughter, Ch. Dandyhow Burnished Silver being very dark all over, with a silver and copper thread running through their coats, and jet black masks and ears when young. Unfortunately, the black shades became white very early, but this is still a most attractive colour.

The colour also varies with the coat growth. My Ch. Barn Owl is quite a light grizzle with her new coat, becoming darker until she is dark-backed, and then, as the coat dies, she becomes lighter again. When stripped to her undercoat she is red! Very confusing to anyone who does not understand Border coats and colour, and as both these conditions wax and wane constantly, one can only conclude by saying "very confusing".

17   Ch. Titlington Tatler, born 1919, considered the best there had been up to that time. Although very short of face-furnishings in this photograph, the strength of his head is still evident.

18   Ch. Bladnoch Raider (by Revenge), with Ch. Not So Dusty. Two very famous Borders bred in 1932, and both owned by Mr. J. Johnson who owned a very strong team in the 1930's.

19   Ch. Future Fame, sire of seven Champions—A name which appears in most pedigrees. Born 1948.

20   Another well-known sire, Monsoon, owned by Mr. and Mrs. G. R. Benson, and bred in 1958 by Mr. R. Morrison from his good bitch, Xmas Box by Montime, a son of Ch. Billy Boy and the famous brood bitch, Jessabelle.

21 Mrs. S. Mulcaster's Ch. Portholme Magic, 1946, showing perfect balance.

22 A well-coloured blue and tan, Dr. and Mrs. Cuddigan's Ch. True Temper, aged 5 years, born 1953.

23 Ch. Happy Day, owned and bred by Mr. J. T. Renton, note particularly the refined otter head, and the racey hindquarters. Born 1959. Ch. Happy Day won best of breed at Bellingham Show for 3 consecutive years. Weight 15lbs.

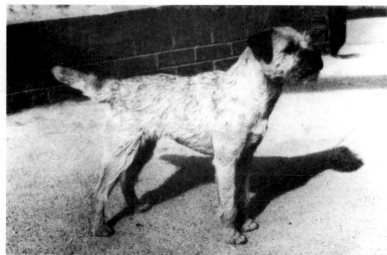

24 Ch. Newsholme Modesty, bred by Miss M. H. Vaux in 1967, owned by Mrs. M. Sneddon. Miss Vaux's first champion was whelped in 1927.

CHAPTER 10

Breeding

Anyone owning a nice bitch will sooner or later think of breeding from her, for various reasons. They may want a successor to her, or they may be interested in breeding show or working dogs, or both. Or they may have heard that they must do this for her health. My advice to anyone who asks me whether they should breed for the latter reason is always the same, and that is that there is always a considerable risk of losing one's bitch, therefore it is not worth taking this risk for fun. Personally, I do not enjoy breeding Borders, for this reason, and if I could find someone willing to breed them exactly to my blueprint, I would gladly never breed another puppy.

However, the breed must go on, and luckily for it, not everyone feels as I do, though every experienced Border breeder knows the anxiety over each whelping. By some strange quirk of fate, the novice breeder usually has good luck for the first few litters bred. Then, when he becomes more serious about it the troubles very often start. When I have been bemoaning the fact that breeding Borders is not easy, with graphic descriptions of the disasters which I have experienced in this field, I have often been the recipient of pitying looks from people who have bred one or two large and flourishing litters with no complications, who have even insinuated that I must be the complete idiot not to be able to do likewise. However, these people have, without exception, all said to me at a later date that they had thought I must have been doing something stupid but now they were experiencing the same

141

problems. Lest this sounds too discouraging I must point out that the fact that there are somewhere around one thousand Borders registered with the Kennel Club every year means that it is possible to breed them, even if it is a rather haphazard process. This is definitely not the breed for money-spinning brood bitches who are expected to pay the electricity and rates bills. A bitch may produce a large and trouble-free litter and then for her next litter need a Caesarean operation or lose several of her puppies through fading. The Veterinary bills, the stud fee and the cost of rearing the puppies well to a saleable age, eight weeks, may well total more than the value of a small litter.

Breeding a litter is a most time consuming operation. To breed and rear a litter well one must not skimp on the time given to the puppies by the breeder, or on rearing on the very best food available. Nothing but the best is good enough when rearing livestock of any description. Once the litter has arrived it is essential that the breeder spends lots of time just looking at them every day. By doing this one will spot any trouble before it starts, both with the whelps and the brood bitch. As the puppies grow older one must just stand and stare at them as they play to see which has the most personality, who is the underdog, how they move and their general style and deportment. Of course it is also necessary to play with them and handle them so that they form the bond of friendship and trust with humans. The actual labour of preparing meals, feeding and cleaning out their kennel takes much more time than one expects and one should be prepared to devote this time to a litter before embarking on breeding it.

The selection of the stud dog needs most careful thought. The choice lies between an outcross, line breeding, or in-breeding.

An outcross will appeal to the novice, who will have heard and read dreadful propaganda in the Sunday papers

every year around Crufts time, about the dreadful mons-
trosities produced (apparently on purpose) by dog
breeders. When using any dog, one puts onto the puppies
the good and bad points of that dog—not speaking
genetically but in very simple terms—and not only of that
dog, but of his ancestors. Therefore, by adding another
complete set of names, one is introducing all the bad of
all the dogs, as well as all the good. Remembering that
one only needs a little bad to spoil an otherwise good
dog, there seems to be less chance of eliminating the bad
by adding more and more different sorts of bad.

Line-breeding is the safest form of breeding, as roughly
speaking, one breeds into a line that is already proved to
be fairly safe without introducing too much outside
influence. The danger of this for a novice is that very
often they will pick the name of a well-known Champion
and collect his blood, without knowing his virtues and
faults, and forgetting that he also had a mother, who
may have been nothing special, and that they are also
collecting her blood!

In-breeding is for the experts only. This is in fact
purifying the strain, as by breeding very closely one brings
out the good and the bad. Should the bad predominate,
there is no point in continuing, but should the good come
out, the breeder knows this to be more than just chance.
This is an excellent way of clearing a fault from a strain,
but a long process and with a high wastage when used
for that purpose. I repeat again that in-breeding is not
for the novice, as one must know the ancestors very well,
and all their pros. and cons. before embarking on this.

Genetics I do not intend to enter into here, as there are
excellent books upon the subject, particularly by
Dr. Marca Burns and Dr. Fitch Dagleish. However, I
should like to stress here that in simple breeding, two
wrongs do not make a right—i.e. by mating short legs to
long legs one does not produce the right length of legs.

The novice would be well advised to take the pedigree
of his bitch either back to the breeder, or to the owner of

one of the dogs or prefixes which appear close behind the bitch, and of course the bitch herself for the breeder to see. These people will nearly always be willing to help. At a very recent show, a novice did this to me, with a bitch sired by a dog I bred. After looking at her bitch and studying the full pedigree, I suggested two Stud dogs as possible mates, of two different lines which appeared in the pedigree, both excellent Champions. To be sure that I was not advising the lady wrongly, I called in the breeder of another grandparent on the pedigree. She studied the bitch and pedigree thoughtfully, and then suggested the two same dogs, much to the amazement of the owner of the bitch.

The dog having been decided upon, it is advisable to ask the owner whether it will PLEASE be possible to bring your bitch. This should be done tactfully, as there seems to be an assumption that the owner of any dog can be made to use their dog at stud, and that stud dogs are the property of the breed. I myself find it difficult to remember that they are not common property when making my breeding plans.

The bitch should then be watched carefully for signs of coming on heat. The first sign will probably be an enlarged and rather damp-looking vulva, and any dogs around her showing signs of interest. This will be followed by a blood-coloured discharge. The bitch must be kept in, and away from any neighbourhood Cassanovas, who at this time will find a way into, under, over, or through almost anywhere the bitch is kept. A brick building with a key and a grid on the window is the ideal 'purdah'— failing which, a travelling box which can be purchased for a few pounds can provide a safe place to keep her, in your kitchen. It will not hurt her to be confined in here for a few weeks, provided she gets plenty of supervised exercise.

Having made an appointment with the stud dog owner to visit the dog between the eleventh to thirteenth day, it is wise to check your bitch to see whether she is ready from the ninth day onwards. By walking a dog (if there is one handy) up to the bars of her kennel one can test this, as the bitch will come to the bars and cock her tail at him, if ready. In the event of there not being a dog handy, pressure from your hand on the back at the root of the tail is just as good a test. Should the bitch be seen to be 'standing', i.e. cocking her tail, before the date arranged, the stud dog owner should be contacted and arrangements made to take the bitch there as soon as possible. One of mine stood and was mated on the second day, producing a fine litter of seven puppies.

Needless to say, the bitch should be perfectly fit at this time, free from disease, including the cough which is the present day bugbear, and of course free from skin trouble or vermin. She should also be not too fat, so if on the plump side should be dieted a little beforehand.

A well fitting collar and lead are required, as the owner will be required to hold the bitch firmly on this, so that she cannot bite the dog, and a loose fitting collar will not contain her for a second if that is her intention.

The mating of Borders is not easy, as a general rule. When we first came into the breed we were rather horrified at the lack of proficiency on the part of the stud dogs, it sometimes being a very chancy affair. For this reason, I would advise a novice to use a dog from one of the better known kennels, if possible, as we have found that these dogs, and their owners, are more experienced.

I do not propose to discourse at great length about stud dogs and their management. There are plenty of other books which deal with this aspect of the dog-game in great depth. Unless a dog is truly outstanding or has some very outstanding virtue or bloodline, it is not really worthwhile for a novice to keep him, or any other breeder for that matter. Only really top class dogs attract much stud work. It is disheartening to have a reasonably nice dog which no one will use. The kennel space is better occupied by a bitch of the same standard, who can then be mated to a top class dog to raise the standard a little.

The dog puppy must never be discouraged from his interest in sex, either by a cross word from a human or from the bitch which he may be bothering. They are easily squashed when young and this could stop them from mating a bitch later when required to, if they think there will be trouble.

The dog should be kept fit and not too fat. When he is about ten months old he could mate his first bitch. Ideally an older brood bitch, who can show him the ropes and encourage him, is the perfect choice for a first mate. Inexperienced dogs can be terribly stupid and a bitch who knows all the tricks can often give him a nudge in the right direction at the right time.

Once the dog has penetrated the bitch it is advisable to hold him up on her back for a few minutes before gently trying to turn him around, as sometimes the "tie" is broken at this stage. It is advisable to have two people to help with any mating, if possible, as then one has control of the bitch and the other of the dog.

Some dogs resent their "wives" being held by humans. This quirk is rather irritating when the bitch is awkward or bad-tempered. Therefore it is better to start as you mean to go on, and to handle the very first bitch.

Dogs that are regularly used at stud are more likely to be proficient stud dogs, and fertile, than the pet dog or older inexperienced dog. I have found that the best stud dogs have been those in the kennels of the top breeders, for this reason, and because they are started right. It is extremely disheartening when one has carefully bred the litter on paper, to find that the chosen dog refuses to mate the bitch. This has happened to me on several occasions with my Borders. I wonder what would have happened if my breeding had gone as planned, not by a series of eliminations.

I do not like my bitches running loose with the dog. Any courtship can be done just as well with the bitch held on her lead. After a preliminary frisk, the bitch should 'stand' to the dog, whereupon he will mount her.

It is now up to the owner of the bitch to keep a tight hold on the head of the bitch, as she is very likely to try and swing her head round to have a nip at the dog when he 'gets home'. Some Border dogs are trained to mate their bitches on a table, others on the floor. The stud dog owner will have control of the business end of the dog and bitch. Should the dog be unable to penetrate the bitch, this can often be achieved by altering the levels, either by moving about on the natural slope of a slight hill, or with the use of a plank, rolled up mat, or even in extreme cases shallow steps. Lowering and raising the bitch's head will also help to alter the level very slightly. Once the dog has penetrated the bitch and is safely 'home', they should tie, however a lot of stud dog owners will keep the dog up for as long as possible before allowing him to turn around and come down off the bitch, as he can very often slip out whilst doing this. The owner of the bitch must see that the bitch is not allowed to roll on the dog, a naughty trick they sometimes try, which can damage the dog badly. The tie will last anything from five to forty-five minutes, so be prepared for a long wait. Once the dog comes away, I pick the hindlegs of my bitch up, standing her on her front legs for a couple of minutes: maybe an old wives' trick, but I still do it just in case it helps! Then I take her to the car, and settle up with the owner of the stud dog.

Sometimes one may have to leave a bitch with the owner of the stud dog. I do not like this, as I like to see the matings myself to know whether I am satisfied. However, it is usually safe to assume that the well-known and reputable breeders will take good care of your bitch. Sometimes they will give a second mating, the following evening or morning, but they are not obliged to do this. One good mating on the right day, achieved with co-operation from the bitch, should be satisfactory. More than one mating spaced further apart than the following day is not recommended, as then the owner of the bitch does not know when the puppies are due, and can often delay getting veterinary help with the whelping through this.

It is usual to pay a fee immediately after the mating. It is inexcusable to leave without paying this fee. Sometimes the stud dog owner may arrange to take a puppy in lieu of fee, from a particularly nice bitch, or in special circumstances to help the owner of the bitch, but they are in no way obliged to do this. For myself, I always pay the fee, as I am breeding every litter to have the pick of it myself.

The bitch must continue her purdah until all signs of her being interesting have gone, usually about three weeks or a little more after showing the first colour. Care should be taken to see that she really is ready to meet the 'wolves' again.

No special care is needed for the in-whelp bitch for the first four weeks or so, apart from normal good feeding and plenty of exercise. I would not advocate exhausting her to her limits working at this time, or dragging her to long distance shows. From four weeks the meat and protein in her diet should be increased.

Approximately four and a half weeks after the mating, the bitch will start to show visible signs of her impending litter, after her dinner. By five weeks she should be showing in-whelp all the time. As she gets larger and heavier, she may become rather lazy. However exercise within limit is good for her; she should not be allowed to become soft in condition or fat.

A suitable place should be arranged well in advance of the litter. It is helpful to have an infra-red lamp for the puppies; this should be fixed up before the whelping, suspended very securely by a chain so that it cannot fall onto the puppies, and so that it can be heightened as the puppies grow to need it less. The puppy kennel should be warm and draughtproof. Often, the puppies are whelped in the breeder's bedroom or bathroom, and then moved out to their regular accommodation once it is seen that all is well, probably after 24 hours.

The whelping bed should be one that the human element can see and reach into with ease. Some are chest type boxes with a lid, others are open boxes. The type I use is an open box, inside measurements 1′ 10″ x 1′ 6″, with a wooden ledge nailed around the inside about three inches from the floor, so that the bitch cannot squash her puppies. The bed is thoroughly disinfected and dried out in the sun well in advance of whelping, as is the kennel if the litter is to be whelped outside. No "nosy parker" dogs are then allowed inside the whelping kennel.

Every breeder should purchase a bottle for feeding tiny puppies well in advance of their first litter so that this is immediately to hand should an emergency arise. Once the crisis is upon you, the time wasted telephoning around the local dog breeders for such a bottle and collecting it from them could well mean the difference between life and death to a tiny puppy.

About eight and a half weeks after the first mating the bitch is watched for signs of whelping. The usual signs are picking at her dinner, anxiousness, digging holes under kennels or hedges and a slightly wild expression. Enlarged mammary glands are another sign. Any long hair around these and the vulva should be cut off at this stage. Should the bitch go over her time (sixty-three days or nine weeks to the day of the mating) the Veterinary Surgeon should be consulted.

I introduce the bitch to her whelping bed by making her sleep in it with the infra-red lamp, very high, turned on to accustom her to the arrangements. Newspaper is put in to line the bed which the bitch will turn into confetti and arrange into a rough nest once the puppies are imminent.

The infra-red lamp is invaluable to tiny puppies but should be used with caution. Water should always be available, both for the bitch to drink and to keep the atmosphere moist. The lamp must not be too low over the bed as it can burn the puppies and the bitch. The snag to the lamp is that the use of it can mask symptoms of distress in the bitch. If she pants it is difficult to assess whether she is merely too hot or whether she may have retained an afterbirth or even another puppy. Also, sometimes the bitch may leave her puppies if she does not like being under the lamp herself.

Once the bitch shows signs of whelping she should be put into her whelping bed. There will be a great deal of activity by way of tearing up newspaper, pacing around, panting and probably whining before she settles down to have the first puppy. I try to keep an eye on the proceedings without fussing the bitch. A perch is made where I can sit well back from the whelping bed, very still so as not to distract the bitch, but so that I can have a clear view. Bitches very often whelp in the early hours of the morning, so be prepared for a disturbed night. Have the Veterinary Surgeon's telephone number on a pad near the telephone . . . . just in case. The paper tearing, bed-making stage can go on for some time, so one need not be there all the time; I just keep an eye on the proceedings. Once the bitch starts to have her first puppy, it is advisable to be in attendance. The infra-red light should be on at this stage.

The bitch will start to strain, very often running around her apartment in a rather frantic state. If she cannot be coaxed back to her bed, I keep an eye on her. She should give birth to the puppy within an hour of the first contractions, and most certainly should not be left for more than two hours without the Veterinary Surgeon being summoned to help. It is always awful to have to call him out at night, but should the bitch be in need of a Caesarean sector, it lessens her chances of survival if she is allowed to become exhausted. The head and feet of the puppy should appear first, and with a few more contractions from the bitch, the whole puppy should be emitted, complete with placenta. If the puppy comes wrong way round (a breech birth) the bitch may need simple assistance quickly.

150

To remove a puppy, make a good lather on your hands and wrist with soap and water, and as the bitch strains, gently ease the puppy downwards. Great care should be taken not to hurt the bitch, if in doubt the Veterinary Surgeon should be called in. If a novice can procure the services of an experienced breeder to show them the ropes at a first whelping, unnecessary calls to the poor Veterinary Surgeon could be saved, as very often a puppy can be helped out with experience. Also, an experienced breeder knows just when trouble is starting and whether something unusual is happening.

Border bitches usually bite the bag open to free the puppy, lick it clean, bite through the umbilical cord and eat the placenta, but they should be observed to be doing this. If they do not free the puppy, the bag should be opened with a pair of sterilised scissors, and should the cord not be cut, this should be done about an inch away from the puppy's body. Once the puppy is clean and tidy, it should be seen to be suckling—a guiding hand to the teat may help it here, although I do not like to interfere unnecessarily as the bitch can become fussed. The puppy and bitch should be in the bed together now.

Should the puppy appear to be dead, showing no signs of life as the bitch licks it, I take over trying to revive it. My methods may be primitive, but I reckon the puppy cannot be worse than dead, whatever I do, and it may be better if I can make it breathe. I drop it from hand to hand playing ball with it, massage it in a towel, breathe gently into its mouth, all of which have 'started' apparently dead puppies. Once it has gulped and is breathing, I return it to the warmth of 'mum' as soon as possible.

The puppies may arrive in quick succession, so that poor 'mum' has scarcely time to tidy up one arrival before the next parachutes out. Should the clean and dry puppies appear to be pushed out and neglected, they can be placed in a cardboard box or basket, under the infra-red lamp, or a warm, but not hot, hot-water bottle under several layers of towel, which is placed on the bottom of the box or basket. It is very imperative to keep small puppies warm.

With a very large litter, the bitch may take a long break halfway through and have a snooze. This is good for her to regain some of her strength, but should she not resume whelping after a few hours, and there are obviously still more puppies, the Veterinary Surgeon should be called in.

Once she has settled down with her complete family, I remove any very wet newspaper, give the bitch a drink of milk ãnd sugar, and leave her in peace to sleep it off. The infra-red lamp should not be too low over the puppies, never lower than about four feet, and there should always be a bowl of water in the kennel for the bitch, as otherwise she may become dehydrated.

The bitch will not want to leave her puppies, but must be made to go out and spend her penny after a few hours when I change the newspaper in her absence. She should be observed carefully for signs of anxiety, or prolonged panting, as this may mean she has retained an afterbirth, and the Veterinary Surgeon should be called in to give her an injection, if so. The bitch will have a discharge from the vulva for about a fortnight—which will colour the newspaper green.

For the first few weeks she should be watched for signs of eclampsia. Panting, staring eyes, looking at the puppies with an intent face ('watching' the puppies) or carrying them around and trying to bury them, are all symptoms of this. Again, the Veterinary Surgeon should be called in, as an injection will put this right. Failure to do so could result in disaster to the bitch and the puppies.

Borders do not usually have large litters, the ideal being between four to six puppies. Bad whelpings often occur where there is just one or maybe two puppies, who are large and wellgrown on all the goodness that should have gone into the whole litter, I have heard it said that bad whelpings in Borders are caused by wide skulls, but have not found this to be true in my experience. The over-sized puppies stuck by their shoulders have been the cause, and inertia of the uterus another cause. One or two litters of nine and ten have been bred and reared, but I think six puppies quite enough for a Border, seven I would maybe leave, but after that would definitely put down some puppies. As I require bitches, I would remove the dogs first, and anything with white toes, or any tiny bitch puppy. Although puppies reared from large litters often appear perfectly reared, I think it is hard on them when they in turn become brood bitches, as they may just not have had sufficient calcium to be able to pass it on to their puppies, and so both they and their puppies suffer, and so do the next generation. For this reason I condemn breeding from any bitch on two consecutive seasons without a very good reason for so doing.

The puppies should go on normally now. The bitch will require light food for the first few days, and four light meals a day. This usually consists of brown bread and milk, and sugar (or glucose), no red meat but a little chicken or rabbit if available, and an occasional egg, calcium and Vitamin D being added to the meals.

Fading puppies are the next hazard. What causes this we do not really know, although varying scientific reasons are given. A squalling puppy with a flattened appearance, away from the others is the first sign of this. Nothing that one can do will save that puppy, and it is better to let it die quickly rather than try to save it, (although of course one always tries—human nature being what it is), as for one thing the bitch will be anxious about its whining and may neglect the good puppies by fussing over this one. Very often a novice will say 'and the bitch lay on one', this is the fading puppy. The anxiety of this for an experienced breeder is how many more will follow. This happens any time up to three weeks old. A Veterinary Surgeon may be able to prevent more puppies from fading with injections.

Another sign to watch is noisy puppies through the bitch's milk having dried up. An injection can start the flow again if spotted quickly. The teats should be felt every day anyway to see that they are all soft, and checked to see that there is milk. Should the glands be hard, some milk should be gently drawn off by hand, but should this condition continue, again a Veterinary Surgeon should be consulted. With a large litter, the breeder should sit and see that every puppy gets a turn at the milk bar, as sometimes the less strong puppies may be pushed out.

Puppies that are doing well should be silent except at feeding times, or when disturbed. Contented grunts are the best sound to a breeder's ears.

It is important to note that Borders tails are NEVER docked. The dewclaws may or may not be removed. A working dog does use them and need them to use as a thumb when climbing and scrabbling up and down rocks, walls and steep banks. For pet dogs they can be a trouble as they may need cutting, otherwise they can grow in a semi-circle and back into the leg of the dog. Should they be removed, this should be done by a Veterinary Surgeon a few days after whelping.

The eyes of the puppies will begin to open at around ten days old, and they will take a bleary look around. Quite soon afterwards they will begin staggering about, coming up onto their legs. The puppies should be handled (with clean hands) by the breeder from an early age to become used to this.

As soon as possible after the eyes are open, try to feed the puppies, as this will relieve some pressure from the bitch's resources, and lessens the likelihood of eclampsia. To do this, start them on Farex, not too sloppy, not too stiff, no lumps, luke warm. The puppies are placed right up against the dish, and a little Farex rubbed on their mouth with the fingers, which they will lick off, and then come for more. Gradually drop your fingers into the dish, so that they are licking the Farex in the dish, and off they go. It is amazing how quickly they learn this. For the first few days they have a meal morning and night, but as they become hungrier (very quickly), this is increased to four meals. Minced meat is added, also Calcium and Vitamin D. After roughly the first packet of Farex, change them onto two meals of puppy meal, (size number one), and two of Farex, the meat being served for breakfast and tea with the biscuit meal; lunch and supper (last thing) being Farex. The mother at this stage should be having a good breakfast (with vitamins and meat), a drink of milk for lunch, (and as a treat for supper), and her normal teatime "dinner" of terrier meal and meat. I find that the bitches like this late night "supper" visit, and after they have had their meal and spent their penny, they like a chat to show that they are really still the favourites, although the puppies may be getting the attention. I always admire the puppies too, and tell the bitch how lovely they are.

At about three weeks old the puppies should be wormed with a special wormer for very young puppies. I use Earlyworm, which really shifts the worms at this stage. The bitch should be kept away from the puppies until they have produced their individual piles of worms, and these have been cleaned up and burnt. No starving is necessary with this wormer, but should one be used that requires the puppies to fast beforehand, a light meal should be given after worming before resuming the usual diet.

Puppies should not be outfaced by large amounts of food, they should leave the dish polished with licking, but also be well filled, but not over-filled themselves. I hate to see puppies with food in their kennel. Personally, I do not like to rear my puppies on "complete foods" as I like to know what my puppies are eating, and to add the vitamins myself. At about three weeks, I change the very fine puppy meal for a "Junior" meal.

Once the puppies start to get up on their legs, they will quickly become mobile and start widening their horizons. They will soon be clambering out of their bed, and they should be shown the way to climb back into the bed, usually up some brick steps placed against a corner until they can manage the climb without them. Make them go up these steps several times each, although they will grumble at such treatment, then hope that they will have the sense to go back into the bed with mum themselves.

Toenails should be cut from a fortnight onwards, and not allowed to become long as they will scratch the poor bitch underneath when feeding if this is allowed. Cutting the toenails of a puppy regularly, not forgetting the dewclaws, up to the age of about six to eight months, usually means that these will remain short for the rest of the dog's life, although of course they should be checked at intervals throughout the life of the dog.

The infra-red lamp should be raised gradually. From ten days or so, depending of course on the condition of the puppies, I try to turn this off for half an hour, and gradually increase this period of time, until the puppies are only having it at night, and then not at all. Infra-red is invaluable to small puppies, and in the first few hours can be vital, but I do like to turn it off as soon as possible once the puppies are thriving.

The bitch will have stayed with her puppies and virtually have to be prized away from them for the first few days. After about four days she should be encouraged to go for short walks, and will soon want to go for her normal walks with the other dogs. Care should be taken that she does not start a fight on returning to her companions, and also after her walk, when she will dash back to the door of her puppies' kennel, and see-off the other inquisitive dogs.

As soon as the puppies start to lap, she should be removed for an hour in the morning, and an hour in the afternoon, this time being gradually increased. She will feed her puppies and clean up after them, and of course sleep with them at night, but if she cannot get away from them she may become bored and irritable with them, as they can pester the bitch as they become more active.

A bench which she can jump up onto away from her puppies is useful after the first couple of weeks.

Assuming that the weather is not too damp or cold, I try to move my puppies to an outside kennel as soon as possible, once they have dispensed with the use of the infra-red lamp. This should be turned off completely for at least a couple of nights before attempting to move the litter. The bitch will, of course, still be sleeping with the puppies at this stage.

The kennel should be dry and warm, free from draughts and the bed should be easily accessible to humans, for ease of cleaning. The puppies are moved when the day has warmed up a little, and the bitch goes with them. All are then shut into the sleeping compartment for the first day, and night. The following morning, provided the weather is not damp or chilly, the door of the sleeping compartment is opened, and a safe grid fixed across this, so that the puppies cannot wander outside. The bitch resumes her routine of visiting the puppies at regular intervals. After two or three days, the grid is removed, so that the puppies may venture out in their own time. Should there be a steep step back into the sleeping quarters, a brick should be put so that they can clamber back. A board should be placed on the concrete run, so that the pups can sit on this in the sun.

Free playing outside in sunshine is essential to young puppies, to develop both their characters and muscles. However, they should never become exhausted, and should be put back to sleep after a good gallop and romp. An old hearth or scrubbing brush makes a welcome toy.

At about six weeks, the bitch should leave her puppies. She should have reduced her visits to morning and evening by this stage, for a quick feed for the pups, and should not sleep with them now. Neither party will like this at first, and there will be howling on both sides, but one must harden one's heart as she must cut the apron strings sooner or later, and sooner is better than later for her sake.

However beautiful the bitch may be, she will look ghastly at this stage. The coat will start to fall out—this can be helped by stripping—her back will be hollowed and her spine sticking up as she may be painfully thin, having given her "all" to the puppies, her quarters will be pinched and her undercarriage hanging down. To build up the bitch again, she will need plenty of exercise, a breakfast of good food with plenty of meat and vitamins, and a good supper. The puppies must not be allowed to suckle her now, as the flow of milk should be drying up and will continue longer should the puppies persist. It is a good idea to worm her when she has left the puppies. She will still take a proprietary interest in the puppies for some time, and may regurgitate her own meals for them, either to them, or outside their kennel if she cannot reach them. This must not be allowed, as the bitch must retain all her food to build up herself. It is difficult to prevent, but the bitch should be led past her puppies and shut firmly in. My April Mist would regurgitate for her daughter, The Cuckoo, until eventually I parted with Cuckoo at two years old!

The puppies will need worming again at around seven weeks old. For this I now get something from the Veterinary Surgeon, as these worms are stronger and take more shifting than the first time. The pups should also be powdered against lice, as it is amazing how they will pick these up.

When the time comes to sell a puppy, it should be healthy, wormed, de-loused, have it's toenails and dew-claws cut, and have a completed pedigree, registration certificate and signed transfer form.

From the age of seven or eight weeks onwards the puppy will start to lead the life which it will lead as an adult either as a housedog in a new home or as a kennel dog.

Ideally it is easier to run on two puppies which are living outside for a few months as they provide both company and central heating for each other. A single puppy at this age will miss the warmth from it's litter brothers and sisters so great care should be taken to see that it has a very snug bed. A soft furry toy or old hearth brush provides a good stand-in for the companionship of the touch of the litter, but not of course for the warmth.

By this time the puppy can gradually make the transition onto more adult food; remember to go through this for lumps which should be removed. At about three and a half months the diet should consist of breakfast, an adult supper and a drink of milk or egg and milk at lunch-time. The vitamins are fed on the breakfast meal. Gradually the change-over onto the full adult diet should be made by the time the dog is six months, with maybe still a small breakfast until eight months. This really depends on the puppy. The art of rearing is to know by instinct precisely which day is the day to make the next step in the chain of progress.

The inoculations should be started by the time the puppy starts to change it's teeth. This is most important as, should the puppy experience a reaction to the inoculation with a high temperature, the second teeth could become stained permanently as a result. This is known as "distemper marked teeth" and is unsightly, although I do not think a dog should be penalised in the showring for them.

Twelve and a half weeks is the earliest that a puppy can start the course of inoculations. Provided the puppy is fit and well it is advisable to start this as soon as possible, so that the course is completed in advance of the tooth changing.

The milk teeth generally start to fall out at about four months. This is a time when the progress of the new teeth should be watched most carefully and is an anxious period for experienced Border breeders, who learn never to "count their chickens" until they are over this stage of development. The first teeth (milk teeth) have roots which are dissolved by pressure from the second teeth (permanent teeth) from the rear. Should the second teeth not come directly behind the first teeth they will pierce the gum elsewhere, and the first tooth will remain. Attention should be paid to this and should this happen the first tooth should be gently loosened with the thumb-nail. If it does not come away after a couple of weeks it should be removed with forceps, as it can cause trouble in the gum.

In my experience, apart from mouths where the bottom jaw is really undershot, quite a few poor mouths are caused by the chance order in which the teeth change. Nothing can be done to alter the actual order but should the bottom teeth grow faster than the top ones a little help can be given by pressure with the thumbnail. This will only be required for two or three days at the most, three or four times per day. The young teeth are fairly movable at this stage and gentle pressure, after opening and shutting the mouth to make sure the teeth are correctly placed, does help. Once the top teeth are over the lower ones they should continue to come in the correct manner. Should any milk tooth be pushing a second tooth into the wrong place, that milk tooth should be speedily removed.

I spent many an hour in my early Border days with puppies with wry mouths on my knee, pushing their teeth back. This proved to be a total waste of time and effort as the teeth always came wrong again. Now if I see that formation starting I let nature take it's course.

Once the teeth have all changed and settled down, at about six months of age, they should require no more attention during the normal course of events than an occasional glance to see that they are all there. I have had more than one nasty shock during these routine checks, particularly after my mother had been looking after my best Champion in my absence and had not been able to resist, quite rightly, the chance to work her. She did not dare tell me what had happened until I enquired why my precious bitch had a tooth missing!

Some dogs may require the tartar removing off their teeth from time to time in adult life. This tartar is caused by the saliva of the individual animal so some are more prone to it than others. This is a very easy thing to remove with the aid of a small pen-knife. Starting at the top of the gum and working downwards towards the point of the tooth, by inserting the tip of the pen-knife under the yellow encrustation on the tooth, it is easy to scale this off. There is a knack to this which is very easy to learn and I have found that, provided they can sit on my knee, the dogs don't mind at all.

From six months onwards the adult dog should require little extra attention, apart from stripping the coat, attending to toe-nails and dew-claws, worming, de-fleaing, powdering the ears for canker, keeping a check on the anal gland should the dog be prone to discomfort there, and scaling the teeth from time to time.

Should it appear off-colour in any shape or form this should always be treated seriously and veterinary help should be consulted early.

CHAPTER 11

Judging

If you have persistently appeared in the showring with good stock, and behaved in a sporting and civil manner, the day may come when you will be invited to judge, maybe a match meeting or maybe a few classes for the breed at a smaller show. The idea may fill you with instant terror, but do not refuse without thought. This is an honour, and you will not have been asked unless someone thinks you are capable of fulfilling the requirements. Also, it is a fascinating opportunity to find out about dogs, firsthand, which one has only seen from the ringside.

So, if you feel you would like to try, accept the invitation by letter, stating clearly any expenses or fee you may require. Then forget about it, do not lie awake at night pre-judging the dogs or worrying about who may or may not be there; there is no point in this, as everything is so different once one is in the ring. One discovers the most surprising things on handling dogs, so that it is useless to try and pre-judge them. Before the big day, do, however, LEARN the Standard thoroughly, so that you can recall any paragraph accurately and easily. I always read the Standard twice the night before the show, and again in the morning, each time as if I have never seen it before, so that I know what the Standard says, and not what I think it says, or would like it to say!

Arrive at the show in good time, so that there is time to report to the secretary your arrival, have a snack, and generally make yourself comfortable and as tidy as possible. Ladies, remember you have to bend down, so please check that you are decent when doing so, in your smart outfit. Gentlemen, please pin that tie firmly down so

162

that it does not flap in the dogs' faces. And do remember
that it might rain and the Borders may be judged out of
doors, so be prepared!

Go to the ring at the time appointed, do not panic,
your mind will probably be blank at this stage, your
knees knocking and your teeth chattering. Introduce
yourself to your stewards, find your pen and prepare for
action.

When the first class has assembled, mark off those
present and those absent in your judging book (which
will either be given to you by the secretary or will be
waiting for you with the steward in the ring, the former
being the most usual procedure). Take a good look at
the dogs as they stand in the ring, noting their general
type, balance and expression at this stage. Then, if you
want to do so, send them round the ring a couple of
times. Although this is not really necessary, the exhibitors
like it as it gives their dogs time to either limber-up, or
settle-down, depending on the character of the individual!
Note how the dogs move, whether or not they have a
forward action with drive, their tail carriage and general
outline. Do not become confused by them going around
too often. Stop the leader as it approaches your judging
table for the second time, and indicate that you would like
the dog on the table. Most judges do, although there are
some very experienced specialists who prefer to judge
them on the ground, maintaining it is infra-dig for a
working terrier to go on a table—a logic which I cannot
follow, as surely these same people examine a puppy on
a table before purchasing it. It is also extremely awkward
and uncomfortable for both judge, exhibitor and dog to
be grovelling about on the floor. Wherever you are judging, up or down, allow time for the dog to adopt its best
position, as one wants to see the best in the dog, not the
worst. Start at the head and work backwards over the
dog, examining each point carefully, in the same order
on each dog so that you do not overlook anything, and
silently conjure up the Standard as you do so. Having

reached the tip of the tail, go back to any point that worried you and look again, by look I mean not only with the eyes but also with the fingertips, which tell one so much about a dog. Never on any account be rough, this is unforgivable, and a way of making sure there will be no exhibitors next time. I, personally, span and lift the dog to try it's balance, replacing it on the table, although many judges lift the dog down to the floor to see how it lands on its feet, whether balanced or top-heavy. For some reason I do not like this done with my own dogs, I have no idea why unless it dates back to a judge picking up and dropping from a height one of my bitches, three times, (to prove what I never asked), so I do not do it myself.

Then ask the exhibitor to move the dog, either straight up and down, or in a triangle, i.e. up one side of the ring, across the top, and back towards the judge on a diagonal line. I like them to go straight up and down twice, the first time to see the dog moving directly to and from me, and then I move to the side of the ring, to see the movement from the side, both sides of the dog. Several dogs which I have judged over the years go very well when viewed from one side, but not so well from the other—and I have discovered it is almost impossible to make the exhibitor do a triangle and then reverse it. I have found it much simpler to go to the side of the ring myself to view both sides of the dog in action.

Having judged the dogs individually, have another look at them, try to choose your prizewinners for positive virtues, not by fault judging, as the result will be better this way. One can end up with mediocrity at the top if fault judging. Do not look for onces that remind you of your own "Lass", similarly, do not think of the handlers, the breeders, the pedigrees, what any one else would do or think, just try and put up the best according to the Standard, which is not necessarily the one in best coat, with the best head, or the best shower. You are there to find the best DOG.

When assessing the virtues and faults in any dog one must try not to get carried away in either direction by one's personal fads and fancies. It is the over-all goodness that one wants. Some Border judges in the past judged entirely on head and coat condition and payed little or no heed to whether the dog could walk or not. Any fool can judge the biggest head, as I fear that was what was considered the best head at one time, and also the best coat condition, but it takes a judge to judge the best dog.

My personal fad is tails. I loathe to have a bad tail in my kennels and am always very aware of my own dogs' tails. However, when judging I take the tail into consideration of the Border as a whole, as do I the head and coat. The actual condition of the coat does not concern me greatly provided that there is evidence of the correct textured top coat and undercoat. Once after judging I was hauled over the coals in a very gentle way by an exhibitor who remarked that I could not have been thinking of his bitch when I wrote the report stating that she had a good coat, as she was shown very out of coat. In actual fact her coat was correct in texture and showed evidence of an undercoat, therefore to my mind the bitch has a good coat, although it may have been short on that one occasion.

If it is a big class, pull out those that you like, and then sort them out. Place your final winners clearly in the centre of the ring, not at the side of it as this is contrary to Kennel Club rules. Mark your book, and make notes on your winners for your report. No need to dot the "i's" here, use a shorthand of your own. My book reads something like "+ type, move, coat, +Sh. —bone and feet, + +head and expr." which then appears in the report as "lovely type, super head, expression, ears and eyes, sound mover, a shade light in bone, feet could be improved, clean shoulders, in good double coat." Having made enough notes in my own code to recall the dog, I can then remember other things about the dog which I have not written down.

Should the novice judge be struck with mental paralysis after going over the exhibits, which often happens, the best thing to do is to make a move of some sort. You may be struck with the thought that they are all marvellous, or all dreadful, or just that they all look alike and there is nothing outstanding. Make a decision on something, to sort the sheep from the goats. Having thus made a definite move, either to send out the discards or to short list the ones you like, it will then be much easier to judge the others. The great thing in this event is to do something, the dogs do not alter as you stand and stare at them!

Never place a dog for any reason except that it should be placed there. There is only one correct solution to each show for each judge, and your job is to achieve it; not to think that poor Mrs. So-and-So hasn't had much luck lately, or this little girl deserves encouragement, or how can I go on leaving out all this exhibitor's dogs, he's given me such a good entry and come such a long way, and really should be in hospital, not here at all.

People have the strangest ideas about judging. The judge has one task only to perform and that is to place the dogs in order of merit, according to his interpretation of the Standard. To place the dogs for any other reason is dishonest. I have known judges boast of their own integrity by stating that they never put up one of their own dogs or one bred by them, never put up their friends, try to make the prizes go around the exhibitors, like to find a new dog to put over the established dog of the day, try to do the novice exhibitors well, do not put up the big names etc. etc., all of which divert the judge from what should be his single-minded purpose, to find the best dog.

For fear of sounding a paragon of virtue, I am sure that I am not alone when I confess to having running through my brain, as well as my thoughts on the dogs and the Standard, what I can only describe as a long-playing gramophone record recorded by Satan himself, of

166

the most ghastly thoughts similar to those above, which I totally ignore apart from finding rather an amusing companion. Should one give in to this, havoc would result, and I for one would never be able to live with myself again. I often wish I could relay it loud and clear to the exhibitors—and then think perhaps they would not be amused. Let us hope that science never progresses far enough for them to be able to tune in!

In each class, make sure that any dogs which have come forward from the previous classes are standing on a different side of the ring to your 'new' dogs, and that they are standing in the order in which you placed them. Never trust the steward; good ones are a tower of strength to a judge, but not infallible, and any judge worth his mettle should be able to manage the placings. After judging your 'new' dogs, go straight back to your 'old' dogs, and look at them again, then return to your 'new' dogs. This way you do not forget your 'old' dogs, and also they get a fair crack of the whip as you are reconsidering them all against your 'new' dogs who after all, need not necessarily be better.

As you progress through the classes, keep a look out in each class for your winners from previous classes, so that you do not lose them. Exhibitors can be very vague about where they stand, and it is up to the judge to keep his winners in sight.

For myself, when faced with a close decision, I have several ways of sorting the placing, apart from the anatomy and type of the dog. I imagine the dog trotting out at the heels of a pack of hounds—either it looks right for the part, or it does not. Then I think which would I buy FOR WORK—and always before I decide a major award, I look at the dogs and say to myself "which of these dogs am I robbing if I do not give it this award?" This I find solves the problem finally, leaving no shadow of doubt as to which is the better dog, personal preference being removed.

167

Some judges will try to make a line-up of the same type. As one is looking for the outstanding specimen, this seems illogical, as if there is a super dog there, he must win, and it is extremely unfair to penalise him because no-one else has brought one similar. There can be several variations in type, all answering the Standard equally well. To my mind all should be given credit for this fact, even if they do not look alike, and the best should be selected from them. Ideally, one would of course like to be able to select a line-up of excellent specimens, all of the type one prefers—but this is just a piped-dream—the numbers of excellent specimens being comparatively less than that of the also-rans. That is why we still try to breed an outstanding animal.

A point which is sometimes raised is that a judge should be thinking of the Terrier Group ring when judging. To me this is a most dangerous thing to do. The judge should be judging to the Border Terrier Standard and only to that Standard. A good dog for a variety class need not necessarily be the best Border as showmanship, slick presentation and sometimes definite breed faults will carry a deal of weight under some judges. For instance, a Border with a short back, sprung ribs and high set tail could well look good to a "Terrier" judge who might not understand that we require the deep and rather narrow rib-cage, more length of back and slightly lower tail set than, say, a Wire Fox Terrier. Should we start breeding specifically for Best In Show wins the breed could well become just another "Terrier" shaped dog. I am not decrying Group and variety wins; they are most creditable and must be for the good of the breed, provided that they are judged on true breed merit.

Once you have finished your classes, and made your best of breed award from your unbeaten dogs, and any other specials which have to be decided have been judged, make sure that you have not retained any award slips in your judging book which should have gone to the secretary's office (it is amazing how often one finds the final slip in the book when one does the report at home!).

The real nightmare of judging follows the actual judging with the report for the dog papers. From experience I have found that I just cannot attempt to write this the evening of the show as my mind cannot recall the dogs at all. However, the following day I can recall the dogs quite clearly. The actual writing takes several hours for a big show. I like to complete the report and post it the day following the show, and then I can resume my normal everyday activities. Should I not be able to write the report the next day it hangs over me until I have posted it. Once posted, I forget about the report, the show and my placings.

It is advisable to keep a careful record of all classes judged, as the Kennel Club requires this information should your name ever go forward for a Championship Show. It is easier to have a neat list in your kennel record book, than to turn the house upside down looking for catalogues from six years past!

Before judging a Championship Show, it is advisable to have judged as many classes for the breed as you can, over many years, and in different districts. At Open Shows, the more local exhibitors tend to support, and as type varies a little from district to district, one wants all the experience of going over these rather different dogs before embarking on a Championship appointment, where dogs will come from every part of the country. A Championship Show judge does hold a position of responsibility and this task should not be undertaken before sufficient experience has been gained at lesser shows. Unfortunately we have had some judges accepting these appointments too early in their judging careers, and thus making the mistakes that all judges make whilst feeling their feet, on C.C. awards. It is much better to refuse the invitation until one has had plenty of experience, than to make a fool of oneself at an important level, and do untold harm to the breed.

After judging a show, do remember to wash your hands most carefully before touching your own dogs at home — it is easy to bring back germs to the kennel on your hands, clothing and shoes from any show. This should become an automatic habit on returning from a show, hunting or even afternoon tea parties where one may have been petting the housedog. One cannot be too careful.

CHAPTER 12

The Border Terrier Overseas

Although the Border Terrier originated in a comparatively small area of Great Britain, it gradually spread throughout the islands and then crossed the Oceans to foreign parts. The principal countries of adoption to date are Sweden, the United States of America, followed by Holland, in order of strength and numbers. The breed is also known in Canada, more recently in New Zealand, and in many other countries throughout the world there are small numbers of them.

Sweden is definitely their second country. They seem to understand the Swedes, and they them, and are becoming increasingly popular there. The breed pioneer was Mrs. Anna Bergman who imported from Mr. John Renton in the late 1930s Happy Thought and Saucy Queen. Happy Thought became an International Nordic Champion, and Saucy Queen must surely hold the record for being the oldest member of her breed ever to become a Champion which she achieved at the ripe old age of eleven years! These two bred only one litter, of which only one puppy survived an outbreak of distemper; this was the first Border owned by Miss Julia Geijer and won two C.C.s. He sired some puppies from imported bitches, but the breed was not popular at that time and the line died out.

They were re-introduced in 1940 by Baron Leijonhufvud importing several, amongst them Tweedside Red Joker and Raisgill Risky. The breed struggled on but made little progress.

However, from the Baron, Miss Brita Donner purchased a puppy which gave her a love for the breed. She herself later imported several very good dogs, and from then the popularity of the breed waxed strong. Her prefix is Monkans. Amongst those she imported were Sw. Ch. Leatty Golden Linkup and Sw. Ch. Leatty Golden Randy, and from these she bred Int. and Nordic Ch. Monkans Tico Tiko, winner of Best in Show at the Swedish Terrier Club Championship Show in 1965, and Swedish and Finnish Ch. Monkans Trapper, owned by the Stafbergs. As Miss Donner is a Finn who resided in Sweden for some years, she played a large part in popularising the breed in both countries.

Trapper sired five Champions including one very famous one. This was Int. and Nordic Ch. Bombax Ericus Rex, the first of the breed to win Best In Show All Breeds at an all-breed Championship Show in Sweden, and I think in the world. This he did at the largest show there had been in Sweden up to that time, The Swedish Kennel Club Show in 1964, under Mrs. de Casembroot. He was owned at that time by Mrs. Bergman, and had been presented to her by Brita Donner and Julia Geijer as a token of their gratitude to her for re-introducing the breed to Sweden.

Also imported by Miss Donner were Sw. Fin. Ch. Todearth Blue Jacket, who sired five Monkans Champions, Sw. Ch. Leatty Golden Randy, Jessica of Tharhill (sister to Ch. Leatty Juliet of Law), and Eignwye Editor who was owned in partnership with Julia Geijer.

Gunnar and his son Carl Gunnar Stafberg imported Sw. Ch. Leatty Panaga Tess, in whelp to Smokey Cinder, which bred Int. and Nordic Ch. Bombax Despot—the dog who twice won Best In Show at the Border Terrier Club of Sweden's Club show, under John Harrison and myself. From Miss Donner they had Sw. Ch. Monkans Mikron which mated to Trapper bred Int. and Nordic Ch. Bombax Ericus Rex and Nord. Ch. Bombax Erica. This kennel has owned and bred too many Champions to list, but mention must be made of a very famous one, Int. and Nord. Ch. Toinis Mikko, a grandson of Despot. Mikko's wins are legion, including two Terrier Groups and Reserve Best In Show at an all breed Championship Show. From England came Daletyne Danny Boy and Felldyke Bonnie Hinney, both sired by Daletyne Rory, and also Eng. Ch. Foxhill Fulbert, Eng. Ch. Clipstone Guardsman, and Clipstone Clover—all of whom have gained further honours in Sweden with their titles. Carl Gunnar Stafberg was a most welcome judge at Leicester Championship show in 1974, the first Swedish specialist judge to officiate in England.

Toini Helleman purchased Bombax Freja from which he bred Int. and Nordic Chs. Toinis Jessika and Mikko, and from Bombax Erica, Ch. Toinis Pami.

Another import of note was Wharfholm Winsome-Moore, a very typical bitch who achieved the unique distinction of becoming a Working Terrier Champion. She is by Wharfholm Harranby Topper ex Ch. Wharfholm Wayward Wind.

Miss Julia Geijer (Juniper prefix) bred her first litter in 1963, although of course she had owned the breed in its early days in Sweden. This litter produced for her Sw. Chs. Juniper Myrra and Minta. From the Bombax kennel she purchased Sw. Ch. Bombax Erica. From England came a very important dog, Sw. Ch. Wharfholm Warrantop, full brother to Ch. Mr. Tims. He has sired many Champions in Sweden; again the Juniper kennel has too many to list. A few years later, Eng. Ch. Mansergh Rhosmerholme Amethyst was imported in whelp to Ribbleside Robert The Bruce. This was a repeat mating of a litter which Julia Geijer saw in England and liked in the nest. Again this proved a judicial move, as a host of champions appeared from Amethyst and her descendants. After this litter she was mated to the established Swedish bloodlines, and to Daletyne Danny Boy, and produced good ones each time. Two sisters of Ch. Dandyhow Shady Knight were the next imports.

173

Crister Gellanson imported Sw. Ch. Llanishen Ivanhoe, a dog who was sadly missed in England as he was one of the best dogs by Shady Knight and left our shores before he really had time to make his mark either as a show or stud dog. England's loss being Sweden's gain, he has produced some outstanding stock. Crister Gellanson became very keen on the working side, which had been rather neglected, and is busily promoting this aspect of the Border which must be in the best possible interests of the breed. He is working them to fox and badger.

Farmway Seagull and Sw. Ch. Hanleycastle Rebel are amongst recent imports to make their presence felt.

The Border Terrier Club was founded in Sweden in 1962, and there is a very close link between the Swedish and British breeders. It is not unusual to have Swedish visitors to the Championship shows and touring the kennels, and of course there are always several overseas visitors at Crufts.

The first Border Terrier in Holland was an import from England in 1932, a dog named Sandyman of Kandahar, owned by Mr. Jüngeling. The following year Mr. Harms imported a dog, Southboro Stanzo, which became the first Dutch Champion, and a bitch. There was then a long interval when no Borders were imported until Mrs. Langhout imported some in the early 1950s.

Mrs. Ploon Wetzel de-Raad, noted for her Tassel prefix in Cockers and Borders, purchased a puppy from the only two Borders there were in Holland, Raisgill Rego and Glenluffin Red Queen, owned by Mrs. Langhout. As a mate for this puppy, Eng. Ch. Golden Imperialist was purchased, and these two bred three Champions including Tassel's Red Queen. Then Eng. Ch. Braw Boy came to Holland, and like Golden Imperialist, became an International Champion. He died, however, after siring only one litter, two years after his purchase. To replace him as a mate for Golden Imperialist's daughters, a son of Ch. Winstonhall Counden Tim, called Winstonhall Dunkie, was purchased. This proved a most successful stud dog as he sired the type liked by Mrs. Wetzel de-Raad. A daughter of Dunkie and Red Queen was mated to Ch. Tedhars Traveller from Germany.

Another kennel of note in Holland is that of Mr. and Mrs. Bons de Weever, whose prefix is Roughdunes. The original stock for this kennel came from Mr. Hall's Deerstone bloodlines. More recently the blue and tan Dutch and Belgium etc. Ch. Wharfholm Wickers Walkabout was added.

An interesting record has been kept of the litters bred in Holland. In eighteen years a total of sixty-seven litters were born, giving an average of 3.8 puppies per litter.

De Nederlandse Border Terrier Club was founded in 1971 with a membership of 77 which has been doubled in five years. As there are comparitively few shows in Holland the enthusiasts travel abroad to shows and make their dogs International Champions under the rules of the F.C.I. By these rules the dog must win four C.C.s in three different countries, from three different judges, over a period of twelve months. Although Borders have been placed several times in Groups in Holland, one has yet to win a Terrier Group.

Hunting of foxes with dogs is illegal in Holland, so it is not possible to work the Borders, as the only form of hunting allowed is drag-hunting. However the breeders endeavour to maintain the stamp and temperament of a working dog on their Borders.

In 1929 a pair of Borders arrived in Canada from England. The bitch was Mr. Smart's Twempie Tinker. These were owned by Mr. Patterson of Buck Skin Ranch, which is situated some 4,000 feet above sea level. These dogs lived in outside kennels where they slept in temperatures of 40° below Zero. These two produced a litter of four puppies in 1930.

The present leading enthusiast in Mrs. June Monaghan (formerly Watson). Reared in Lancashire, she had Borders from her earliest childhood. The first one she owned in Canada was Can. Ch. Bucksmoor Emma, bred by Mrs.

Symon, which arrived from England in 1954. The following year Deerstone Docker, brother to the famous Ch. Destiny, arrived to join her, and he gained his Canadian title. Then followed the C.C. winning Can. and Am. Ch. Glenluffin Pomona, Can. and Am. Ch. Deerstone Damsel and Can. Ch. Deerstone Danby who gained a Companion degree, the first of the breed to do so in Canada. From Mrs. Marchant came Hawkesburn Badger and Hawkesburn Foxglove. Badger and Damsel bred Am. and Can. Ch. Birkfell Bobber Burrills, who had many Group placings, and Can. Ch. Birkfell Penelope. Ch. Birkfell Baroness Mischief came from Danby and Damsel. Mr. Mosle from U.S.A. mated Baroness Mischief to his Eng. Ch. Falcliff Tantaliser producing Can. Ch. Town Hill Teacup of Birkfell, owned by Mrs. Monaghan. From Mrs. Kate Seeman, U.S.A., Mrs. Monaghan purchased another dog by Eng. and Am. Ch. Deerstone Debrett and Am. Ch. Deerstone Tylview Dusty, namely Can. Ch. Shelburne Trigger. Mrs. Monaghan and her daughter are great enthusiasts for the promotion of the breed, and travel tremendous distances to attend shows both in Canada and the United States.

Mrs. Ruth Hussey bred Can. Ch. Buckhurst Flicker and Can. Ch. Buckhurst Lark, from imported Farmway stock.

Other notable imports were Eng. Ch. Leatty Lucky, Eng. Ch. Lily of The Valley, Can. Ch. Maxton Medallion and Mr. W. Veitch's C.C. winning dog, Day-A-Head who I believe was never shown in Canada.

At one time large firms in Canada imported Border Terriers from England to give to important customers as status presents. Luckily this craze was short-lived.

The Border Terrier Club of Canada was founded in 1973. In two years the entry at the breed Booster show showed an increase of nearly 150% which is an indication of the increasing enthusiasm for the breed. Apart from the interest in shows, there is a great interest in Obedience in Canada.

Germany has never been a stronghold for the breed, but there have been a few Borders there for some years. The most notable would be Mrs. Steen's Eng. Ch. Deerstone Dugmore, who has won his title in several countries and been placed in terrier groups frequently—he has been a great ambassador for the breed on the Continent. Mr. Ted Harper exported several who did well, German Ch. Tedhars Traveller being another well-known dog.

Mrs. Mulcaster sent a lovely bitch to Denmark, Portholm Monawen, who became a Champion there, but I do not think the breed is very popular there yet. There have been a few in Italy, Miss Long's export Winstonhall Wish Well being one of the only Champions there for many years. A few went to Switzerland, but again did not really make a mark, however, there seems to be more interest at the moment with enquiries for them as working dogs. In France there are a few, again chiefly workers.

The Border has been a registered breed in America since 1929, although eighteen had been exported from England prior to that date including Eng. Ch. Rustic Rattler in 1928, which Mr. Percy Roberts bought intending him to be a show dog. However the dog proved to be such an excellent worker that he never reached the show ring, being busily occupied in other directions.

From 1929 a few Borders of good English bloodlines were registered. Mr. Massey registered the first two American-bred litters in 1931, both sired by Mullach (Arnton Billy—Arthorne Lady) out of Always There and Dryffe Judy, the latter a daughter of Ch. Station Masher. Mr. Massey exhibited eleven Borders at his local show in 1935, including Knowe Roy and Red Twister (Twempie Tony—Eng. Ch. Todhunter).

Am. Ch. Pyxie O'Bladnoch, in whelp to Ch. Fox Lair, was imported by Mr. MacBain, and produced Diehard Sandy, who sired Am. Ch. Diehard Dandy. Mated to Red Twister, Pyxie bred Diehard Betta, the dam of Am. Ch. Diehard Dandy. The line produced many more

177

winners and worked in very well with the later imports. The earlier lines apart from this one died out through the years.

Amongst other early imports of note were Eng. Ch. Share Pusher in 1938 and Eng. Ch. Gay Fine in 1940, Emigrant of Diehard (Eng. Ch. Dipley Dibs ex Wind o'Lammermuir) and Bladnoch Blossom (Red Sunset ex Bladnoch Maeve) and Heather Sandy of Diehard (Fearsome Fellow ex Tishy). The latter two went over on the same boat in March, 1942, and evidently enjoyed the sea-air and a shipboard romance as Blossom produced a litter in May, much to the astonishment of her owner! These puppies had typed on their Registration Certificate "Bred at sea, whelped in U.S.A.".

Mr. Latting (owner of Am. Ch. Diehard Dandy, Bladnoch Blossom and Am. Ch. Heather Sandy of Diehard), Mr. W. MacBain (owner of the first American Champion, Pyxie o'Bladnoch of Diehard and importer of Heather Sandy) and Dr. Merritt Pope were the chief enthusiasts in the early 'forties.

Dr. Merritt Pope co-owned with Mr. MacBain Am. Ch. Druridge Imp of Philabeg, 1944, and bred his first American Champion, Philabeg Red Miss, in 1946 from Diehard bloodlines.

From Red Miss's daughter, Am. Ch. Philabeg Red Bet, bought by Margery Harvey and Marjory Van der Veer as a puppy, came the first of the many champions registered with their prefix, Dalquest, Am. Ch. Dalquest Dangerous Dan. He was sired by Dronfield Nick, a dog brought to America by the brother-in-law of Capt. Gorrell-Barnes of the Dronfield prefix in England. This gentleman, Capt. John Nicholson, aroused the idea of a Border Terrier Club in America, the foundation meeting of which was held at the Westminster Show in 1947.

Dr. Pope and the early members drew up a Standard, with advice and help from English breeders, which was approved by the American Kennel Club in 1950, and an excellent Standard it is, too. More explicit than the

English Standard, it differs in only one respect and that is the tail-set, "not set on too high"—whereas it is required to be "set-high" in the English Standard. The weight is the same as in our Standard.

Mrs. Kate Seeman, formerly Mrs. Kate Webb, imported many top class Borders from England. The first was Eng. and Am. Ch. Lucky Purchase, from Mrs. Mitchell's Cumberland kennel. From Sam Ormston came Am. Ch. Golden Fancy, who produced many American Champions, amongst them the first Shelburne bred one, Am. Ch. Shelburne Slipper born 1952. Many of Britain's very best Borders arrived in this kennel including Am. Ch. Chalkcroft Blue Peter, Eng. and Am. Ch. Dandyhow Bitter Shandy, Eng. and Am. Ch. Brieryhill Gertrude, Eng. Ch. Rab Roy, Eng. and Am. Ch. Jonty Lad, Am. Ch. Covington Eagle, Am. Ch. Dandyhow Sarah, Am. Ch. Deerstone Tylview Dusty, Am. Ch. Daletyne Red Admiral, Eng. and Am. Ch. Deerstone Debrett, Am. Ch. Deerstone Decorum, and Eng. and Am. Ch. Dandyhow Shady Lady. Besides this illustrious list, there were a host of home-bred American Champions bearing the Shelburne prefix. The dogs from this kennel were worked by Mr. Webb.

The Dalquest Champions are legion. Apart from those made up by their breeders, many are made up by other people. The foundation bitch, Am. Ch. Philabeg Red Bet was bought in 1947, and the first Champion was bred from her, in 1948. From Mrs. Mulcaster were imported Am. Chs. Portholme Marilda, Max Factor, Meroe, Mhor and Bellarina. An important bitch here was Am. Ch. Dour Dare, by Dangerous Dan out of a Tweedside bitch, bred by Mr. Beckett. Dour Dare with Max Factor produced at least five Champions. About 1965 Am. and Eng. Ch. Portholme Macsleap arrived at Dalquest, a well-known sire in England and a lovely dog. He proved a good sire for the American bloodlines too, producing many Champions. Mated to Am. Ch. Dandyhow Schnapps (full sister to Eng. and Am. Ch. Mansergh Dandyhow Bracken) he produced at least three Champ-

179

ions for Dalquest, Chevinor Maria of Dalquest is another import to gain her American crown for this kennel.

The Cinjola kennel of John and Esther Barker from Indiana started with Am. Chs. Dalquest Dauntless and Dare's Dancer, bred at Dalquest in 1957. Mated together these produced seven Cinjola Champions. From this mating, and the introduction of lines from Pearlene Smith's Am. Ch. Raisgill Rosy Girl come many more Champions bearing the Cinjola prefix.

Mrs. du Pont Scott of Virginia, a noted race-horse owner and owner of the famous winner of the Grand National at Aintree, Battleship, imported Am. Ch. Carahall Cindylou in whelp to Ch. Portholme Manly Boy which bred her Am. Ch. Nancy. Cindylou also bred for her Am. Ch. Bruce and Am. Ch. Cronie. Imports here included Am. Ch. Leatty Lucky Gift, Am. Ch. Koffee Lad (bred by Mr. Gaddes), Am. Ch. Cravendale Call Girl, Eng. and Am. Ch. Mansergh Dandyhow Bracken, and Am. Ch. Farmway Dandyhow Likely Lad. Koffee Lad sired Am. Ch. Espresso and Am. Ch. Bull Run, a famous dog who did exceptionally well in groups, being placed at least nine times.

Carroll Bassett, also from Virginia, owned Am. Chs. Dalquest Derry Down, the import Am. Ch. Leatty Jean's Laddie, Ch. Lally, Am. Ch. Toftwood Tarka bred by Mrs. du Pont Scott, and owned and bred Am. Ch. Toftwood Toffee.

Mr. Mosle has had Champions bred in Canada, America and England, including Eng. and Am. Ch. Falcliff Tantaliser. His prefix is Town Hill.

Show and Obedience enthusiasts are Dr. and Mrs. Harvey Pough of New York. Their foundation was Mex. Ch. Dalquest Jody of Townhill who bred Mex. and Am. Ch. Bandersnatch Brillig, C.D. who in turn bred three Champions

Two keen enthusiasts from Chicago, Nancy Kloskowski and Nancy Hughes, who are also interested in Obedience work as well as showing, imported Eng. and Am. Ch.

Workmore Brackon following her win of Best of Breed at Crufts in 1972. The following year Eng. and Am. Ch. Final Honour left for the States, following his great win of Reserve Best in the Terrier Group at Crufts. He is owned by Nancy Hughes and David Kline and is continuing his Group placements in the States.

Dale R. Gourlie has the unique distinction of owning the first ever Group winning Border in the States, Am. Ch. Wattie Irving of Dalquest. Although several Borders had been consistently placed in Groups, this dog did not make the breakthrough of winning one until 1972, a great day for the Breed in America.

Other imports of importance are Eng. Ch. Clipstone Hanleycastle Bramble and Eng. Ch. Workmore Waggoner.

Apart from their position as show dogs, Borders are known in the States for their working ability, where they work woodchuck, skunk and racoon. In some places there are foxes, which are hunted with hounds, but the emphasis is on a good gallop for the horses rather than accounting for the fox—indeed these are carefully preserved to run another day, and a Border Terrier bolting them into the teeth of the foxhounds would be extremely unpopular! It is good to know that Borders are gaining Certificates of Gameness at The American Working Terrier Trials.

The schedule for an American Working Terrier trial interested me: "All terrier breeds small enough to get down a 6 to 9 inch drain including Hunt Terriers and Jack Russells are invited to test their abilities. Earths will be 6 to 10 feet long artificial earths, reinforced. The Quarry will be caged woodchucks—no chance of damage to either chuck or terrier. Sponsored by American Working Terrier Association. Terriers will be judged on eagerness to go to ground, getting down to the game, and baying for at least two minutes. Information for class assignment: Has terrier killed an occasional rat? Has terrier gone to ground to opossum, woodchuck or fox? Has terrier worked as Hunt Terrier?"

Already having celebrated its 25th anniversary, the

American Border Terrier Club has some 118 members from 28 states, as compared with 34 members in 1954, a very healthy, steady rate of growth.

In Obedience qualifications, America must lead the field. Very creditable is the number of Borders which gain either C.D. or C.D.X. awards.

The breed has never really caught on in Eire despite the efforts of Mrs. Swifte (Castleblunden) and more recently Mrs. Phoebe Bennett (Ardcairn). The Castleblunden lines were based on Dipley bloodlines and Mrs. Bennett purchased her foundation stock from Mrs. Sullivan, Dandyhow. Mrs. Bennett worked so hard to popularise the breed and had considerable success herself. The greatest win was that of Irish Ch. Dandyhow Becky Sharpe of Ardcairn (litter sister to Dandyhow Brussel Sprout) who won Best in Show at an All Breeds Championship Show. However, when Mrs. Bennett lost her heart to the Briard, the interest in Borders gradually died down again.

Occasional Borders have been known in Australia and New Zealand over the years, there having been one or two Australian Champions in the past, although I do not think there are many Borders shown there at the present time. Mrs. Williamson has recently decided to boost the Breed in New Zealand. She already had some Borders, including N.Z. Ch. Farmway Swinging Chick, and in 1974 imported further stock of Foxhill, Ribbleside and Clipstone bloodlines. Along with Mr. Jim Graham she is making every effort to put the Breed to the fore, with appearances on Television, writing articles for the Press and by taking good stock to shows, where she is having considerable wins already.

Norway, Austria, East Africa, Portugal, Spain, South America, Bermuda and even the Virgin Islands have, or have had, Border invaders in small quantities, some of whom have shown the flag by becoming Champions, but not really in enough numbers to make a real impact. Sometimes one or two Borders are sold together as workers, and are only too ready to work, whatever the quarry may be!

A daughter of our old Smuts accompanied her owners out to East Africa. A very game worker, she unfortunately met her end through taking on a leopard single handed which proved too strong a match for even the most plucky Border.

CHAPTER 13

Anecdotes

Stories recounting the courage and sagacity of the Border Terrier are found in old articles on the breed, and in modern publications such as Year Books and newsletters. I now intend to tell a few of my favourite stories about Borders, which have interested or amused me for various reasons and which I hope the reader will also enjoy.

My favourite anecdote was told to me by Mr. Russell, M.R.C.V.S. while he was examining one of my dogs during the routine veterinary examination at the entrance to a show. Mr. Russell's father-in-law had a farm on the banks of the Manchester Ship Canal and his Border, Sooty, spent many happy hours rabbiting on the banks of the canal. She also used to frequent the locks and became well known to the man in charge of the lock gates. To the consternation of her owners, Sooty went missing. Her frantic owner searched high and low for her, fearing that she might have been run over, killed by a badger or lost underground. All hope of finding her was given up and the search abandoned, but after six months Sooty arrived home, very excited and pleased to be home, and in perfect condition. Of course, the news of her sudden return spread quickly amongst her friends, who were all delighted she was home. One of her lock-keeper friends remarked that perhaps she had been to Australia, as a ship had tied up at the locks, waiting to go up the Canal to Manchester, that had returned from Australia, after six months, the very afternoon that Sooty had arrived home. The conclusion was that she had probably run up the gang plank onto the ship when it had been tied up waiting for the tide, and her presence not discovered until they were well out to sea, when the only thing to do would be to keep her on board ship until they returned to her locality on the way home to Manchester and could release her in the hopes that she would find her way home.

Another ship story concerned my April Mist who was travelling with me to Dublin, to a show in Eire. She was put into the official kennels on the boat, and bedded-down by me with every comfort for the night, whilst I slept in my cabin. In the morning, we disembarked and travelled to the show. There were not many Borders at the show, and April had a rather distinctive free action which made her easy to distinguish. As we were walking around the showground, a Dachshund exhibitor came up to me and asked if that was my Border. This rather surprised me, and I answered that of course she was. Whereupon I was informed that she had had the whale of a night on the boat with the crew, and had been all round the bars with them, no doubt joining them in a pint!

Evidently Borders take readily to the nautical life. When Mrs. Daykin left Kenya she went to live aboard a 30 foot sloop, taking with her four Borders, ranging in age from fifteen years to one year. During bad weather the dogs were confined to their sleeping quarters but never suffered any sea-sickness or nervousness. None were lost overboard whilst sailing, even though one would lean out to spot dolphins. However they did sometimes fall off when playing on the deck when the boat was at anchor. When this happened they would swim to the rudder and hold on until rescued. In the ports where they were not allowed ashore for quarantine reasons, they would be exercised by swimming with their owners in the harbour, following their owner's dinghy. Very strong swimmers, they became good divers and one even learnt to swim under water for a few feet.

Mr. George Ion sold a Border to a young lady from Northern Ireland. After having had the dog for several years, she took him in her car to Belfast, a place he seldom visited. His owner suspected she had a flat tyre and got out of her car, whereupon, unbeknown to her, the Border also got out. She drove off, and had travelled some distance before she realised he was not in the car, Of course she turned back and searched Belfast, but to no avail. A great search was set up, with the co-operation of the police, but without any results. His photograph was eventually shown on the News on the Television, and the following morning the young lady's cousin phoned to say the dog had followed her to school, at a place ten miles outside Belfast. He had last visited the cousin's house three years earlier, but had found his way there and was waiting on the doorstep when the milkman called. No-one recognised him, so he waited until the cousin emerged to travel to school, and followed her, whereupon he was recognised.

A truly dual purpose Border was Newminster Rummy, owned by Sir John Renwick. This dog made his debut at Bellingham show, where he won all his classes, on the Saturday. The following Monday, the Border Foxhounds met at Bellingham, where Sir John lived at that time. A fox was run to ground in an old quarry, and Rummy was put to ground, where he spent the entire day. He bolted seven foxes, and was badly marked-up as would be expected with so many foxes to ground in one place. The judge of the show was present and was reported as being amazed by it all! Rummy became a noted worker, for many seasons, and sired Ch. Newminster Rose.

Mrs. Owen of Corbridge told a rather gruesome story about her Border, Teddy. She was out for a walk with a friend and they had an assortment of Terriers with them. Teddy was walking with her when the others put up a fox in the open who made to the nearest wood. Teddy, hearing the hue and cry, dashed across and caught the fox, which 'clicked' the dog in the centre of the back and skinned him. Teddy, having despatched the fox, returned to Mrs. Owen whereupon her grandchild then noticed his back. The skin was pressed together from head and tail towards the middle of his back, and bound together with a couple of handkerchiefs tied tightly around his body, and the dog was rushed to the nearest veterinary surgeon, who put twenty stitches into the join and made an excellent job of it. The dog, with true Border dignity, never said a word, but Mrs. Owen's friend passed out cold when the two bandages were removed and the flaps of skin opened out in the surgery.

Mr. Adam Forster's bitch Coquetdale Reward was a grand worker, but in her old age became stone blind. Of course she was not allowed to work after that, but one day she followed the foot scent of Mr. Forster and friends, who had gone out after foxes. When she caught up with them they were busy at a fox-hole. She hunted around with her nose trying to find the hole, and as soon as she found it, went straight in and tackled the fox. Much to the relief of all, they got her out safely.

Mr. Forster was at a local show where a shepherd was showing his bitch, Nailer, and was most annoyed that she had not won. His fury mounted, and after a few drinks, he vowed he would sell Nailer, whereupon Mr. Forster bought her for £2 as a brood bitch. In her first litter she bred Coquetdale Vic and the mother of Ch. Titlington Tatler. All Mr. Forster's dogs descended from Vic.

The great sire Revenge could well have been unheard of but for the 'cleverness' of another shepherd. This man had pestered Mr. Forster for a puppy and eventually he was given the pick of a litter of two, a dog and a bitch. The shepherd chose the dog. After six months a neigh-bouring shepherd visited Mr. Forster and saw the bitch puppy. He then told the first shepherd that he had picked the wrong puppy, the bitch was much better than his dog. Immediately the shepherd came back to Mr. Forster with his dog puppy and asked him to exchange it for the bitch. Mr. Forster took one look at the dog and needed very little persuading: the dog was Revenge. Later that year Revenge was shown by Mr. Forster at the Royal Show at Newcastle, and won, whereupon back came the shepherd to exchange the bitch for the dog again, nothing doing this time!

Coquetdale Vic was nearly buried underground. She was a great worker to fox, and eventually had so much of her jaw torn away that the bone was exposed, but this did not deter her either as a worker or showdog, allowance being made in the show-ring for battle scars honourably won in those days. She was lent for a season to the Border hunt, and was put to ground in a very deep hole with a lot of rubble about. She immediately worried her fox, but could not get out as there had been a fall of rubble meanwhile. The next day a team of workers arrived to dig her out, and after working all day they could just reach her tail and managed to pull her out by it. The next moment the sides of the deep cutting crashed in, filling the place where she had been with rubble.

A six-year-old terrier was sent to hunt-kennels in the South for stud purposes only. The terrier man arrived one morning and collected the terriers for the day's work, a good day's sport was had and on his return to kennels he left a message for the Huntsman to examine Dodger who had been bitten. Dodger was found to be intact, the new stud dog was carrying the battle-scars, and in due course gained his working certificate!

Mr. Dodd's Allen Piper, Tally Ho and Jean are known to have hunted an otter for $2\frac{1}{4}$ hours in the River Mear, eventually killing him, a 17 lb. dog otter—who needs hounds?

As I have said elsewhere, some Borders are death to cats. A bitch of mine was sold overseas, and started her journey from a shipping agent in Skipton. Just before setting off on her long journey she was taken out to 'spend her penny' on a lead. Across her line of vision strolled the king tom cat of the district. This proved too much for Midge, she broke free and set off in full pursuit, out of sight along the streets and alleyways. A frantic

25   Five generations of stud dogs at Dandyhow
Left to right: Dandyhow Cock Robin, Dandyhow Napoleon,
Dandyhow Bolshevik, Ch. Dandyhow Shady Knight and
Dandyhow Brussel Sprout (approaching his sixteenth
birthday at the time of the photograph but still with a
perfect front!).

26   Ch. Hobbykirk Destiny retrieving a grouse at speed
on a Scottish moor, illustrating the aptitude of
some Borders for work as gundogs.

27   Typical Border Terrier puppies,
      Ravensdowne Twig and Twinkle, bred by Miss Fair.

28   A venerable old gentleman, Brookend Vali, enjoying
      a patch of sunlight on the stairs, and listening for his
      master's car.

29   The expert at Terrier Racing, first out of the traps . . . . ..

30   . . . . . and burning up the ground to win every heat.

31   The record-breaking Ch. Step Ahead, winner of four
Terrier groups at Championship shows, and holder of
the record number of C.C.s in the breed.

32   The ends—or a Border's idea of a walk, a nose
into every hole!

chase ensued and she was eventually caught up with and embarked upon her travels, but not until she had polished off that tyrant.

The same person had a well known and very experienced stud dog, Plough Boy, also nuts on cats. This dog was just about to serve a visiting bitch, and actually had the first leg up, when he espied a cat. Giving George one of those telling Border glances that mean "first things first", he dismounted and streaked off after the cat. Having dealt with that crisis, he then returned to his visiting lady love.

My Amethyst, through my stupidity, broke a small bone in her hindleg and was put into a heavy plastercast the same day that she was due to be mated. After much soul-searching, I decided to go ahead, if possible, as the plaster would be off by the time she whelped, and she might as well make some use of her enforced inactivity. The stud dog was very experienced, but took a little time to settle to the idea that a powerful blow from the plastercast was meant as an encouragement from Amethyst. Owing to the rather unusual circumstances, I was not too happy about the mating, which had taken place in a well known joiner and undertaker's warehouse. Throughout the proceedings there had been a vocal accompaniment from a very pretty halfgrown kitten with obvious Siamese ancestry. Bobbie was left to cool off in the warehouse, Amethyst in the car, and we adjourned for a cup of tea. After a suitable interval, proceedings were restarted, and the mating successfully achieved. As I was leaving, Amethyst under my arm, I said "where's that kitten?", at which Bobbie, the stud dog, slunk away in a most guilty manner, ears back, tail down. We searched and searched, knowing the worst but unable to find the corpse. Eventually this was found neatly laid out in a box of shavings, a most professional touch by Bobbie. How we laughed, but not at the fate of the poor kitten who was very special and quite irreplaceable.

Borders can impart information without the use of

words. My Barn Owl, out for a walk with me and the other Borders on a nice summer afternoon at Lilymere, suddenly, for no apparent reason, put her tail between her legs and fled for home, despite my calling her. I hastily followed her, fearing she might be run over by the bread delivery van were she loose in the yard. Just as I arrived at the house, some five minutes after she had left me, there was a terrific thunderclap. The tree by which we had been standing had been literally blasted to pieces, and the lightning had travelled between the two trees scoring a deep furrow in the ground. How she knew of the impending danger I shall never know.

Another of my Borders is a tell-tale-tit. When I am gardening and the Borders are allowed to play around me, but I am not watching their every move, she will report to me with nudges and pokes should anything illegal be happening. One day she nagged and nagged until eventually she persuaded me that I must check up on the others, whereupon I found one had got into my precious guinea pig's hutch.

Recently I purchased an adult bitch who I had sold as a puppy. The first night I made a nice bed for her on the floor next to my bed. In no uncertain terms she told me that she ALWAYS slept on the bed. The battle went on into the early hours, when, for the sake of a peaceful night, I gave her best. I was just dozing off when, with a deep sigh of resignation, she dropped onto the floor and spent the night in her own bed—I proved to be too restless for her to sleep well on mine. Next time I saw her previous owners I checked up on this story and found that it was a complete fabrication on the part of Muffet. She always slept in the kitchen with the cat. Had I believed her fable, and been a more settled companion, I would have had her on my bed for ever I suppose.

My next story is from Mrs. Sutherland, who went shooting with an M.F.H. on his own shoot which the Borders were specially invited to attend. They were looking for a shot pigeon which fell by chance near an

190

artificial earth. One Border, of course, had to bolt a fox, whereupon the other two laid into it and after a savage fight, killed it—in full view in the open. As if this was not enough to ruin the Sutherlands' chances of ever being invited to shoot there again, the other Border was still to ground at a fox. By removing the top stones they dug into her and pulled her out—whereupon to the horror and amazement of all three Borders, the vixen and dog fox were allowed to escape. History did not relate whether the Borders were invited to the next shoot.

A famous Champion Border came to tea with her family at Lilymere, and sat, as good as gold, on the hearthrug glaring into the fire with her back turned on the proceedings. Suddenly, she had an urgent call of nature, and simply had to go out for a second. She came straight back, the tea party went on, and eventually broke up and they all went home, taking Fettle with them. We came back after seeing them off, and started to clear up the tea things, when there was a piercing scream from my mother, and there, sitting on the hearthrug was a very live mouse, clean and dry. No question as to who had brought that in, but how ever did she know it was outside the front door at that precise mement—there were three shut doors between her and the mouse.

Then there is the sporting vicar who takes his Borders to the earth as he goes past on his way to Matins, and collects them on the way home for Sunday lunch!

The aforementioned Smuts was watching the trophies being removed at the end of a hunt where he had bolted the quarry after a long argument with it underground. Suddenly he could bear it no longer and leapt forward and grabbed hold of a large mouthful of skin. My father went on removing pads and tail to give to members of the field, and then tried to remove Smuts so that the corpse could be thrown to hounds for disposal in the time-honoured manner. No amount of burning, choking, ear twisting or swearing would make Smuts loosen his grip one fraction; the eyes were glazed, the jaws locked on his old enemy. The solution in the end was to cut a large circle of skin and flesh away from the corpse, around Smuts' clenched jaws, much to his disgust when he realised how he had been tricked.

A Border puppy called Paddy Reilly crossed the Atlantic in 1925 destined to become one of America's most famous dogs. During his lifetime he collected 30,000 dollars for the Humane Society of New York, helped the police to capture a burglar, on two occasions he gave warnings of fire, he saved three children and a woman from drowning, detected a gas leak and was reputed to have saved a total of 49 human and 9 animal lives during his 14 year life. On his death the Greenwich Village Humane League was founded to his memory.

This last tale is a far cry from the Borders working foxes in the hard Northumbrian hills, but a great tribute to the undeniable courage of the breed, which is proved not only in the famous tales of Titlington Peter and Coquetdale Vic, but also in the routine terrier work performed by the breed daily—courage and guts being required every time a Border meets a fox, otter or badger underground. As an intrepid worker and a loyal and sagacious companion the Border leads the field.

APPENDIX — A

SOME LINES OF DESCENT

Descent in Tail Male (A)

Ginger 1902
Rap
Titlington Jock
Ch. Teri
Riccarton Jock
Burnfoot Jock
Red Rock
Whitrope Don
Knowe Roy
Rab o'Lammermoor
Ch. Foxlair
Callum
Deerstone Dauntless
Ch. Portholme Manly Boy
Fighting Fettle
Dandyhow Brussel Sprout
Ch. Dandyhow Shady Knight
Dandyhow Bolshevik
Ch. Ragus Dark Chocolate
Ch. Ragus Warlock 1973

Descent in Tail Female (A)

Wasp 1910
Jinky 1914
Rita unregistered, 1917
Parkhead Vic
Din Shiela
Miss Shena
Miss Dinah
Dinger Queen
Ch. Scotch Mist
Happy Morn
Lucky Lassie
Border Queen
Ch. Hawkesburn Happy
  Returns
Ch. Hawkesburn Nutmeg
Hawkesburn Linnet of
  Farmway 1974

Descent in Tail Male (B)

Flint (Jacob Robson) 1905
  untraced
Jock unr.
Ch. Ivo Roisterer
Flint
Rab of Redesdale
Rival
Ch. Ranter
Furious Fighter
Fearsome Fellow
Ch. Hepple
Ch. Cravendale Chanter
Ch. Falcliff Topper
Ch. Ribbleside Falcliff Trident
Ribbleside Ringman
Ch. Ribbleside Ridgeman
Napoleon Brandy 1973

Descent in Tail Female (B)

Ruby 1912
Pearl
Spitfire
Teviot Nettle
Jed
Ch. Station Masher
Liddesdale Wendy
Liddesdale Nettle
Stung Again
Finery
Flamingo
Fully Fashioned
Final Flutter
Swift and Sure
Sun Saga
Ch. Kathyanga 1961

Descent in Tail Female (C)

Wasp unregistered untraced
Meg 1918
Kimley Bunty
Jean Wise
Faith
Newminster Wisp
Delight
Daphne's Dream
Joker's Dream

Solar Susan
Druridge Deemstress
Dreamer
St. Keverne Cindy
Sherryripe
Ch. Mansergh April Mist
Mansergh The Cuckoo
Ch. Mansergh Barn Owl
Mansergh Muffet 1972
Mansergh Cushy Butterfield 1975

REFERENCE BOOKS, SPECIALIST AND GENERAL

*Our Friends The Lakeland and Border Terriers edited by Rowland Johns, published by Methuen & Co. Ltd. 1936

*The Border Terrier by Montagu H. Horn. printed by J. Catherall & Co. Hexham.

*Border Lines by T. Lazonby. Published by Shiach & Co. Ltd. Carlisle. 1948.

*Border Terriers by Frank Jackson and W. Ronald Irving published by W. and G. Foyle. 1969.

*Border Tales compiled by Hester Garnett-Orme, published by the Southern Border Terrier Club 1967.

*Border Terrier Champions and Challenge Certificate Winners with all names appearing in a four generation pedigree arranged alphabetically by Hester G. Orme, 1953.

Hunt and Working Terriers by Captain Jocelyn Lucas

Working Terriers by Dan Russell, published by The Batchworth Press, 1948.

Terriers their Training and Management by A. Croxton Smith, published by Seeley, Service and Company Ltd. 1937 circa.

Show Dogs by Theo Marples.

Dogs of the British Isles 1872 by Stonehenge

Dogs In Britain by Clifford Hubbard.

*How to Raise and Train A Border Terrier by S. N. Weiss, published by T. F. H. Publications, 1966, American.

Dogs and How to Breed them by Hilary Hamar published by John Giffard Ltd., 1968.

*Border Terrier Club of America Breed Booklets (published every four years).

*Southern Border Terrier Club Year Books (published annually)

*Newsletter of The Border Terrier Club.

International Encyclopedia of Dogs by Stanley Dangerfield and E. Howell, published by Rainbird Reference Books Ltd., 1971.

The World Encyclopedia of Dogs edited by Ferelith Hamilton, 1971, published by New English Library Ltd.

The Book of the Dog by Brian Vesey-Fitzgerald, Ivor Nicholson and Watson Ltd., publishers.

Modern Dogs by Rawdon B.Lee, 1896.

The Complete Book of the Dog by Robert Leighton 1922.

British Dogs by Hugh Dalziel 1889.

Hutchinson's Dog Encyclopedia 1935.

British Dogs by W. D. Drury 1903.

The Terrier by N.Youatt 1845.

Terriers by Darley Mathieson 1922.

Guy Mannering by Sir Walter Scott 1829.

British Terriers — Kennel Aristocrats — details of publishers not known to me.

An Anatomy of the Dog by Dr. R. N. Smith, 1972 published by Quartilles International Limited — a series of transparent illustrations in colour.

Take Them Round Please by Tom Horner 1975, published by Davis and Charles Ltd., a book on judging.

*denotes specialist books.

Pedigree of Ch. Ribbleside Ridgeman who is line-bred to Ch. Eardiston Fettle, carrying 5 lines to her.

CH. RIBBLESIDE RIDGEMAN

PARENTS	GRAND-PARENTS	G. G.-PARENTS	G. G. G.-PARENTS	G. G. G. G.-PARENTS
Sire Ribbleside Ringman	Sire Ch. Ribbleside Falcliff Trident	Sire Ch. Falcliff Topper	Sire Ch. Cravendale Chanter	Ch. Hepple
				Hevans Sent
			Dam Falcliff Charmer	Hugill Ruffian
				Falcon Jewel
		Dam Deerstone Daybreak	Sire Ch. Deerstone Debrett	Klein Otti
				Deerstone Tinkerbell
			Dam Ch. Browside Rip of Deerstone	Browside Kim
				Browside Gypsy
	Dam Ribbleside Rhapsody	Sire Delphside Descendant	Sire Tod Law	Ch. Future Fame
				Ch. Scotch Mist
			Dam Delphside Fine Fettle	Ch. Deerstone Destiny
				Ch. Eardiston Fettle **1**
		Dam Ch. Eardiston Fettle **2**	Sire Eardiston Sailor	Ch. Golden Sovereign
				Deerstone Dill
			Dam Ch. First Footer	Ch. Future Fame
				Fully Fashioned
Dam Ribbleside Moonmagic	Sire Ribbleside Tagaroa	Sire Klein Otti	Sire Ch. Billy Boy	Callum
				Misty Dawn
			Dam Forrest Skylon	Ch. Future Fame
				Lady Madcap
		Dam Ribbleside Rhapsody	Sire Delphside Descendant	Tod Law
				Delphside Fine Fettle **3**
			Dam Ch. Eardiston Fettle **4**	Eardiston Sailor
				Ch. First Footer
	Dam Delphside Firefly	Sire Nutshaw Bob	Sire Ch. Braw Boy	Ch. Billy Boy
				Lassiebell
			Dam Sporting Lady	Ch. Wharfholm Wizard
				Pepita of Rough Lea
		Dam Delphside Delilah	Sire Ch. Wharfholm Wizard	Ribbleside Rocket
				Ch. Portholme Marthe of Deerstone
			Dam Ch. Eardiston Fettle **5**	Eardiston Sailor
				Ch. First Footer

CH. MAXTON MONARCH

APPENDIX D.   Pedigree showing In-Breeding

Pedigree of Ch. Maxton Monarch who is in-bred to Ch. Future Fame, the only outcross being through Tresta and she carries a line to Tweedside Red Playboy, the Sire of Red Hazel, so is not a true outcross.

PARENTS	GRAND-PARENTS	G. G. — PARENTS	G. G. G. — PARENTS	G. G. G. G. — PARENTS
Sire Ch. Maxton Matchless	Sire Ch. Future Fame	Sire Fearsome Fellow [1]	Sire Furious Fighter	Ch. Ranter
				Romance
			Dam Finery	Gem of Gold
				Stung Again
		Dam Tombo Squeak	Sire Ch. Boxer Boy	Ch. Aldham Joker
				Daphne's Dream
			Dam Cheviot Penny Plain	Reedswire
				Coronation Queen of the Mist
	Dam Maxton May Queen	Sire Ch. Future Fame	Sire Fearsome Fellow [2]	Furious Fighter
				Finery
			Dam Tombo Squeak	Ch. Boxer Boy
				Cheviot Penny Plain
		Dam Maxton Red Princess	Sire Ch. Future Fame [3]	Fearsome Fellow
				Tombo Squeak
			Dam Red Hazel	Tweedside Red Playboy
				Cherry Pye
Dam Ch. Marrburn Morag	Sire Ch. Maxton Matchless	Sire Ch. Future Fame	Sire Fearsome Fellow [5]	Furious Fighter
				Finery
			Dam Tombo Squeak	Ch. Boxer Boy
				Cheviot Penny Plain
		Dam Maxton May Queen	Sire Ch. Future Fame	Fearsome Fellow
				Tombo Squeak
			Dam Maxton Red Princess	Red Hazel
				Ch. Future Fame [6]
	Dam Tresta	Sire Ch. Girvanside Cruggleton Don	Sire Callum	Ch. Foxlair
				Dipley Dinah
			Dam Orenza	Robin Hood
				Madas
		Dam Ch. Girvanside Tigress Mischief	Sire Rodent Lad	Ch. Bladnoch Raider
				Catchburn Maiden
			Dam Barwhin Trixie	Tweedside Red Playboy
				Wimpy